TESTIMONI...

As a Warrior Mom, I have learned to rely on His strength, not my own, to handle everything I am faced with as a mom, wife, and woman. I have become fully equipped to stand firm and strong, to turn it all over to Him, to listen to His truth and focus on His will. And through it all, I am not alone - not only is God by my side, but I have my fellow Christian Warrior Moms to love, support, and pray with. Warrior Moms Unite!

I thank God for The Warrior Mom Handbook; it has blessed my life. It made me aware that I don't have to rely on my own strength, but I can rely on His strength. I learned that through His sacrifice, He has given me life.

Warrior Moms will rock your world!

THE WARRIOR MOM®

KRISTINA SEYMOUR

HANDBOOK

Equipping Women Through the Word

Suwanee, GA

The Warrior Mom Handbook
© 2011 Kristina Seymour.
All rights reserved.

First published by Faith Books and MORE, February 2010

ISBN 978-0-9820197-7-1

Printed in the United States of America

No part of this book may be reproduced, stored in a retrieval system, or transmitted by any means without the express written permission of the author.

Author photo by Andrew Watson Photography

Graphic design by

3255 Lawrenceville-Suwanee Road,
Suite P250,
Suwanee, GA 30024
publishing@faithbooksandmore.com
www.faithbooksandmore.com

❖ ❖ ❖

*To Tracy Henderson, to whom God gave
the Warrior Mom concept.*

*To Brenda, whose artistic talent and love for God provided
the foundation which we built upon.*

To Anne, who constantly encouraged.

*To Nicole, whose obedience to Christ helped transform the unseen
Warrior Mom concept into this book within your hands.*

*To Barbara, whose belief in the Warrior Mom ministry
helped give it wings.*

To Leslie, whose steadfast editing provided clarity and flair.

To Bridgett, whose creativity gave beauty to each page.

*To Libby, whose patience and artistic talent provided
fun, warmth, and strength.*

*To three of the original Warrior Moms:
Evie, Nanita, and Naomi, my forever friends.*

To all Warrior Moms.

*To my loving husband and children,
mere words are not enough to express my love for you.*

And, of course ...

To God, whose love inspires us all.

❖ ❖ ❖

PREFACE

Welcome Warrior Mom to be!

As soon as you made the decision to study how to become a Warrior Mom, your weakness became strength. Now, with the power of God, alongside other women or on your own, a transformation will start! Just like at boot camp, the armor gets issued, the sword gets bestowed, and you begin your journey. Your Warrior Mom Handbook will lay it all out. Each chapter focuses on a particular piece of the armor from Ephesians. Additionally fruit of the Spirit is introduced as we discuss spiritual nourishment. After all, an empowered Warrior Mom cannot survive solely on caffeine and animal crackers! At certain points in the study, you may receive a button representing lessons and victories. As you pin your new button on your Warrior Mom tote bag and reflect on lessons learned, we guarantee that something will begin to happen in you: you will start to feel encouraged, rejuvenated, and strong!

As you begin to study, you will realize that your role is bigger, your influence more profound, and the possibilities for you, your marriage, your children, and your home are limitless in Christ! Hear you roar! You will be prepared, bold, brave, unafraid, and full of faith. You will realize that you are no longer fighting in and with the flesh. No longer will you run in fear, as doubt, defeat and isolated hopelessness bite at your heels like a savage dog. You will stop running, turn, and face the fear, in faith this time, because something has changed in you. Through the dark, dusty, crowded, cluttered room of your defeated soul, a light will come on. God will step in, and as His righteous right hand reaches over you to switch on the light, you will hear Him say, "Are you ready to fight?"

Join other women in a Bible study or invite someone to join you as you study the Word. *Though one may be overpowered, two can defend themselves. A cord of three strands is not quickly broken.* Ecclesiastes 4:12. "For where two or three come together in my name, there am I with them." Matthew 18:20.

Rise up, rise up. God is speaking. Do you hear Him? To women who have been isolated, made vulnerable to the defeat of the enemy, picked on, kicked, and left alone, this handbook is for you. To women who seek God and dare to become warriors, read on. The battle is on and to the enemy's plot against you, we say: GAME OVER!

Love,

God and your fellow Warrior Moms

Warrior Moms Unite! ™

Psalm 139 - wonderfully made

Oh my Heavenly Father,
Please hold me, comfort me, & lift me up!
Our precious child needs your power to overcome the demons he faces each morning & each moment of every day. The demons aren't his to fight alone & help him see that he can depend on others to love him. That the world & especially his family love him & want to protect him & help him healing. Healing is what you can do. All powerful healing. You perform Miracles. You can heal all, Oh Lord. I lift up my child to you. Give doctors wisdom to find an answer to his problems - answers that provide healing. Your love overflows! Fill me up with your love so that it overflows into my son. Show me that sweet, loving boy again with that perfect little nose you gave him. He is such an amazing gift - and you gave him amazing talents. Please, Lord, don't let those talents be wasted. Let those talents be a glorifying of your name because they are yours and yours alone. Just as this little boy is your masterpiece, I give you this

amazing little boy who has brought me so much joy. Flow through him so that he can become joyful again. Dissipate that anger - anger that he doesn't remember. Resolve the anger, calm the anger, destroy the anger. He has a full life ahead that Satan is slowly destroying. Destroy the enemy! You are powerful! You can overcome this for my son. The earth quakes but my soul is calm. You have the power to calm my fears; to make me a mother that can help guide my son through this darkness. It won't be dark here forever. Let your light shine through our lives that lights the path you want us to take. You guide our steps. All these decisions about my son's care is up to you. Show us the right answers. Shower us with your hope and blessings for our son. He is your child and I lift him up to you as a gift. Every perfect gift come from you. Help me appreciate the incredible blessing of that gift. I prayed for this child. Before I prayed for him, you created him. Thank you for allowing me to be his mother. I love you!

2 Tim 4:18

TABLE OF CONTENTS

Preface iv

Chapter 1	Introduction to the Armor of God and Strength..	1
Chapter 2	The Belt of Truth	11
Chapter 3	The First Fruit: Love	19
Chapter 4	The Breastplate of Righteousness	35
Chapter 5	The Fruits of Joy and Patience	43
Chapter 6	The Workout Shoes Fitted for the Gospel of Peace with the Fruits of Kindness and Goodness	49
Chapter 7	The Shield of Faith with the Fruit of Faithfulness	59
Chapter 8	We Pause for an Important Lesson on Arrogance	71
Chapter 9	The Helmet of Salvation and the Fruits of Gentleness and Self-Control	77
Chapter 10	The Sword of the Spirit and Pray in the Spirit on All Occasions	91
Chapter 11	You Must Take Time to Delegate	99
Chapter 12	Yes, We Have an Enemy	103
Chapter 13	Combining the Physical for the Sake of the Spiritual	115
Chapter 14	Don't Confuse all Battles and Wars as Yours	121
Chapter 15	A Very Important Final Point	129

About the Author 132

References 132

Certificate of Completion 135

When Kristina and I met in the summer of '08, we had no idea what God's plans would be for her small group that fall. Over the last year and a half, I have watched the Warrior Mom Small Groups evolve from four women in one living room to numerous small groups that have helped moms, married and single, learn how to be the wives and mothers that God intended them to be. Kristina truly has a heart for the Word of God. This study and the lives it has touched are testimony to her faith and belief that all things are possible through Him.

LISA GOODWIN
SPIRITUAL FORMATION DIRECTOR
WOMEN'S SMALL GROUPS
12STONE® CHURCH

CHAPTER 1
INTRODUCTION TO THE ARMOR OF GOD AND STRENGTH

www.WarriorMoms.net

THE WARRIOR MOM HANDBOOK

CHAPTER 1

No soldier goes into battle without armor. As a Warrior Mom, you must wear your armor and know about its power. Let's read Ephesians, Chapter 6:10-18 to find out what this is all about.

Finally, be strong in the Lord and in his mighty power. Put on the full armor of God so that you can take your stand against the devil's schemes. For our struggle is not against flesh and blood, but against the rulers, against the authorities, against the powers of this dark world and against the spiritual forces of evil in the heavenly realms. Therefore put on the full armor of God, so that when the day of evil comes, you may be able to stand your ground, and after you have done everything, to stand. Stand firm then, with the belt of truth buckled around your waist, with the breastplate of righteousness in place, and with your feet fitted with the readiness that comes from the gospel of peace. In addition to all this, take up the shield of faith, with which you can extinguish all the flaming arrows of the evil one. Take the helmet of salvation and the sword of the Spirit, which is the word of God. And pray in the Spirit on all occasions with all kinds of prayers and requests. With this in mind, be alert and always keep on praying for the saints.

There's a lot to take note of in this passage
1. Our strength does not come from ourselves. It comes from the Lord.
2. We must put on the armor of God.
3. The devil schemes against us.
4. Our struggles are not against flesh and blood. They are not against the people and/or circumstances we see.
5. Our struggles are against spiritual forces.
6. The only way to stand your ground is in the armor.
7. Different parts of the armor represent different things.
8. Pray in the Spirit on all occasions.
9. Pray with all kinds of prayers and requests (not just the big things).
10. Be alert!
11. Pray for others.

For today, let's look at the first point - strength:

Note: I've incorporated a lot of scripture on strength. God impressed upon me that the more we saturate ourselves in the Word, the more it will speak to each of us individually. Therefore, please don't be overwhelmed by all the scripture. Just take it in. You don't have to read it all in one sitting. You don't have to memorize it all. What I want you to get out of this first chapter is this: we rely on God's strength — not our own. That's it. That's the lesson. Please enjoy the following scriptures on God's strength.

Exodus 15:2 *The Lord is my strength and my song.*

Deuteronomy 4:37 *Because he loved your forefathers and chose their descendants after them, he brought you out of Egypt by his Presence and his great strength.*

II Samuel 22:33 *It is God who arms me with strength.*

INTRODUCTION TO THE ARMOR OF GOD AND STRENGTH

I Chronicles 16:11 — *Look to the Lord and his strength; seek his face always.*

I Chronicles 29:12 — *In your hands are strength and power.*

Nehemiah 8:10 — *For the joy of the Lord is your strength.*

Psalms 18:1 — *I love you, O Lord, my strength.*

Psalms 28:7 — *The Lord is my strength and my shield.*

Psalms 29:11 — *The Lord gives strength to his people.*

Psalms 33:16-17 — *No king is saved by the size of his army; no warrior escapes by his great strength. A horse is a vain hope for deliverance; despite all its great strength it cannot save.*

Psalms 46:1 — *God is our refuge and strength.*

Psalms 65:5-8 — *You answer us with awesome deeds of righteousness, O God our Savior, the hope of all the ends of the earth and of the farthest seas, who formed the mountains by your power, having armed yourself with strength, who stilled the roaring of the seas, the roaring of their waves, and the turmoil of the nations. Those living far away fear your wonders; where morning dawns and evening fades you call forth songs of joy.*

Psalms 73:23-26 — *Yes I am always with you; you hold my right hand. You guide me with your counsel, and afterward you will take me into glory. Whom have I in heaven but you? And earth has nothing I desire besides you. My flesh and my heart may fail, but God is the strength of my heart and my portion forever.*

Psalms 84:5-12 — *Blessed are those whose strength is in you, who have set their hearts on pilgrimage. As they pass through the valley of Baca, they make it a place of springs; the autumn rains also cover it with pools. They go from strength to strength, till each appears before God in Zion. Hear my prayer, O Lord God Almighty; listen to me, O God of Jacob. Look upon our shield, O God; look with favor on your anointed one. Better is one day in your courts than a thousand elsewhere; I would rather be a doorkeeper in the house of my God than dwell in the tents of the wicked. For the Lord God is a sun and shield; the Lord bestows favor and honor; no good thing does he withhold from those whose walk is blameless. O Lord Almighty, blessed is the man who trusts in you.*

Psalms 118:14 — *The Lord is my strength and my song.*

Psalms 147:10-14 — *His pleasure is not in the strength of the horse, nor his delight in the legs of man; the Lord delights in those who fear him, who put their hope in his unfailing love. Extol the Lord, O Jerusalem; praise your God, O Zion, for he strengthens the bars of your gates and blesses your people within you. He grants peace to your borders and satisfies you with the finest of wheat.*

Isaiah 12:2-3 — *Surely God is my salvation; I will trust and not be afraid. The Lord, the Lord is my strength and my song; he has become my salvation. With joy you will draw water from the wells of salvation.*

Isaiah 31:1 Woe to those who go down to Egypt for help, who rely on horses, who trust in the multitude of their chariots and in the great strength of their horsemen, but do not look to the Holy One of Israel, or seek help from the Lord.

Isaiah 40:25-31 "To whom will you compare me? Or who is my equal?" says the Holy One. Lift your eyes and look to the heavens: Who created all these? He who brings out the starry host one by one, and calls them each by name. Because of his great power and mighty strength, not one of them is missing. Why do you say, O Jacob, and complain, O Israel, "My way is hidden from the Lord; my cause is disregarded by my God"? Do you not know? Have you not heard? The Lord is the everlasting God, the Creator of the ends of the earth. He will not grow tired or weary, and his understanding no one can fathom. He gives strength to the weary and increases the power of the weak. Even youths grow tired and weary, and young men stumble and fall; but those who hope in the Lord will renew their strength. They will soar on wings like eagles; they will run and not grow weary, they will walk and not be faint.

Jeremiah 9:23-24 This is what the Lord says: "Let not the wise man boast of his wisdom or the strong man boast of his strength or the rich man boast of his riches, but let him who boasts boast about this: that he understands and knows me, that I am the Lord, who exercises kindness, justice and righteousness on earth, for in these I delight," declares the Lord.

Habakkuk 3:19 The Sovereign Lord is my strength; he makes my feet like the feet of a deer, he enables me to go on the heights.

Mark 12:28-31 One of the teachers of the law came and heard them debating. Noticing that Jesus had given them a good answer, he asked him, "Of all the commandments, which is the most important?" "The most important one," answered Jesus, "is this: 'Hear, O Israel, the Lord our God, the Lord is one. Love the Lord your God with all your heart and with all your soul and with all your mind and with all your strength.' The second is this: 'Love your neighbor as yourself.' There is no commandment greater than these."

1 Corinthians 1:25 For the foolishness of God is wiser than man's wisdom, and the weakness of God is stronger than man's strength.

Ephesians 1:18-23 I pray also that the eyes of your heart may be enlightened in order that you may know the hope to which he has called you, the riches of his glorious inheritance in the saints, and his incomparably great power for us who believe. That power is like the workings of his mighty strength, which he exerted in Christ when he raised him from the dead and seated him at his right hand in the heavenly realms, far above all rule and authority, power and dominion, and every title that can be given, not only in the present age but also in the one to come. And God placed all things under his feet and appointed him to be head over everything for the church, which is his body, the fullness of him who fills everything in every way.

Wow! I must pause here for a moment. Did you get that? Ephesians 1:18-23 is for the believer. It makes no sense to the nonbeliever. To the nonbeliever it may as well be Shakespeare. Let's compare:

INTRODUCTION TO THE ARMOR OF GOD AND STRENGTH

ROMEO AND JULIET SCENE IV LINES 96-104

True, I talk of dreams,
Which are the children of an idle brain,
Begot of nothing but vain fantasy,
Which is as thin of substance as the air,
And more inconstant than the wind, who woos,
Even now the frozen bosom of the north,
And being angered puffs away from thence,
Turning his side to the dew-dropping south.
This wind you talk of blows us from ourselves:
Supper is done, and she shall come too late.

LETS LOOK CLOSELY AT THE ARMOR OF GOD

THE BELT OF TRUTH
that buckles around your waist to protect you from the lies of the evil one.

THE BREASTPLATE OF RIGHTEOUSNESS
that protects your heart from being led entirely by emotion.

YOUR FEET FITTED WITH THE READINESS
that comes from the gospel of peace.

THE SHIELD OF FAITH
that extinguishes all the flaming arrows of the evil one.

THE HELMET OF SALVATION
that protects your mind from doubt.

THE SWORD OF THE SPIRIT
which is the word of God.

Granted, I took a piece out of the middle of the play, so it obviously doesn't make sense, but still, Shakespeare's words are full of fanciful ideas and rhythmic melodies. Shakespeare's writing is brilliant and beautiful, but do his words provide life to a lost soul the way the Bible can? When you read the Word, you are fed. Your soul is nourished. Your heart hears it; you drink it in. It provides quenching for the parched soul. It doesn't return void. Shakespeare, on the other hand, requires you to buy the *CliffsNotes* and hire a tutor, and when it's all over, you hope you pass the test, but as far as inspiring perseverance within your soul? No. Shakespeare is incapable of such feats. Oh, but God provides life! The following scriptures come to mind:

Psalms 42:1 *As a deer pants for streams of water, so my soul pants for you, O God. My soul thirsts for God, for the living God.*

Psalms 107:5-9 *They were hungry and thirsty, and their lives ebbed away. Then they cried out to the Lord in their trouble, and he delivered them from their distress. He led them by a straight way to a city where they could settle. Let them give thanks to the Lord for his unfailing love and his wonderful deeds for men, for he satisfies the thirsty and fills the hungry with good things.*

Isaiah 55:10-11 *As the rain and snow come down from heaven, and do not return to it without watering the earth and making it bud and flourish, so that it yields seed for the sower and bread for the eater, so is my word that goes out from my mouth: It will not return to me empty, but will accomplish what I desire and achieve the purpose for which I sent it.*

Remember this: His Word provides life! His Word does not return void. "In the beginning was the Word, and the Word was with God, and the Word was God." (John 1:1) "The Word became flesh and made his dwelling among us. We have seen his glory, the glory of the One and Only who came from the Father, full of grace and truth." (John 1:14) The Word became flesh. God combined the spiritual with the physical through His son, Jesus. And so, I am talking in the literal sense when I discuss God's Word as being able to provide life to you. I mean it in the literal sense.

Open wide the eyes of your heart. There is a strength that has been made available to you in your Bible: the Word of God. And now that we are reminded that His Word provides life, we will continue on in the study of God's strength:

Philippians 4:13 *I can do all things through Christ who strengthens me.*

Hebrews 11:32-34 *And what more shall I say? I do not have time to tell about Gideon, Barak, Samson, Jephthah, David, Samuel and the prophets, who through faith conquered kingdoms, administered justice, and gained what was promised; who shut the mouths of lions, quenched the fury of the flames, and escaped the edge of the sword; whose weakness was turned to strength; and who became powerful in battle and routed foreign armies.*

I Peter 4:11 *If anyone serves, he should do it with the strength God provides, so that in all things God may be praised through Jesus Christ. To him be the glory and the power forever and ever. Amen.*

INTRODUCTION TO THE ARMOR OF GOD AND STRENGTH

In the fall of 2008, a group of women got together to drink coffee, talk about God, and pray. We drank our caffeine trusting that it would provide the strength and surge of energy we would need to plow through the morning and survive the day. We talked about our lives, from five years old to 50 something. We talked about who we were, where we were in our lives, and where we were on our faith journeys. The conversation ended up with us talking about how exhausted we all were. We discussed life: husbands, children, the house responsibilities, the bills, the schedules, the demands, and the depletion we all physically felt. Since we were at a Bible study, however, we got back to the subject of the spiritual. As a result, God in His grace led us to Ephesians 6:10. We knew that if what we'd been doing wasn't working, we should try something else. We got excited about God's armor, and we realized we had been tromping through the battleground of life like turtles out of their shells.

Tracy Henderson, one of the original Warrior Moms, went on a run and God gave her the name "Warrior Moms!" She brought it back to the group and we've been running with it ever since! We found such a sense of relief when we focused on the fact that we don't have to continue in our own strength. We started discussing God's strength: His power, His might, and His faithfulness. If you are as exhausted as we were, focus, focus, focus on the fact that if you trust in God's strength – not yours – you will have an unlimited supply of strength, power, faith, hope and a desire to persevere. You see, *it is not by power, or by might, but by my Spirit – says the Lord Almighty!"* (Zechariah 4:6)

No, it won't be easy, and things won't magically be all better. *"In this world, you will have trouble, but take heart; I have overcome the world." (John 16:33)* I spent a lot of years waiting for things to get better. I waited for that magic, "I've arrived, my family has arrived, my marriage has arrived" moment. I finally realized that I'm never going to arrive because the backdrop of life keeps changing. Therefore, I must learn to roll with it. Just when I thought I'd arrived, my son was diagnosed with Ushers Syndrome, a job change occurred, someone had the flu, a tire was flat, etc. Please keep in mind, therefore, that becoming equipped women of God won't keep struggles five miles away from you at all times. You are in the world so you will have trouble, but this handbook aims to help you become more prepared to deal with troubles in fresh, bold, courageous ways. Please highlight this paragraph. If you're like me, you might even underline parts, put stars next to words, circle certain phrases, and then tape it to your forehead. (Okay, that last suggestion might be extreme!)

Having said that, it's human nature to try to carry all the responsibility and the weight of the world on our "Mom"shoulders. After all, God has entrusted us with so much, and we really want to do a good job with it. Isn't that right, sister? The problem is, we get carried away with one word "we," or "I." If God sent something or someone in your direction, don't act as if you must be God and take all of the burden upon yourself. When God gives you _____ (fill in the blank), don't become a mini god and say, "Oh, this is all mine to deal with." That defeats the fact that God gives it to you, but He only entrusts it to you – to turn it over to Him, and ask Him to help you have the strength to accomplish His will in that situation or that person's life. That was a mouthful. But, do you see? It might have been given to you, but it's not up to little 'ol you to pull it all off. So, rest in God's strength and repeat what a few Warrior Moms repeat to ourselves a lot, "We are simply the vehicles through which God works." Show up in God's strength and yes, give it your all, do your best, but trust God for the outcome. Relax, breathe, and exhale. Welcome to being a Warrior Mom! It entails a different way of thinking.

FIELD EXERCISES

Below, list some things that you have felt were solely your responsibility. List things that have overwhelmed you and made you feel defeated. Below each entry, rewrite it in words that describe how you are going to turn it over to Him. You may simply write, "And I turn _____ over and rely on God's strength not my own."

1. _____
   _____
   _____

2. _____
   _____
   _____

3. _____
   _____
   _____

4. _____
   _____
   _____

5. _____
   _____
   _____

6. _____
   _____
   _____

Additional homework for the rest of the week is to visualize putting on your armor and wearing it. Trust in God's strength, not your own.

INTRODUCTION TO THE ARMOR OF GOD AND STRENGTH

DAILY FIELD EXERCISES

Before you walk out your front door, envision yourself putting on your armor. In Christ you have the belt of truth that protects you from the lies of the enemy; they sound like truth, but they aren't and you MUST know the difference. You have the breastplate of righteousness that is a metal shell that protects your heart from being led entirely by emotion, and it protects your back so that deceit cannot penetrate through your back and pierce your heart when you are least expecting it. Jesus Christ is our righteousness. (2 Corinthians 5:20-21). You've also been given shoes. These represent the readiness that comes from the gospel of peace (Ephesians 6:15). And then, there's your shield of faith with which you can extinguish all the flaming arrows of the evil one. This shield of faith and the protection that if offers allows you to see beyond your circumstances. Satan will fire arrows of doubt and devastation at you to try to defeat you. Your faith allows you to see beyond the circumstance you may be experiencing, past the fear and despair, to the victory that awaits you in the promises of Christ. The helmet of salvation ultimately protects your mind from thoughts of doubt. And finally, you have your double-edged sword, which is the Word of God. It is the one tool that God has given you that immediately puts you on the offensive rather than the defensive. *"And pray in the Spirit on all occasions with all kinds of prayers and requests. With this in mind, be alert and always keep on praying for all the saints."* (Ephesians 6:18)

Warrior Moms Unite! ™

The Warrior Mom Handbook helped me to refocus my spiritual journey as a mom. While in the midst of raising two teenagers, Warrior Moms reminded me that I am not alone in this, that God is ALWAYS near, and that my strength comes from Him and His Word. I have always had the armor... The Warrior Moms' experience just reminded me to put it on!

MARCHETTA JONES
WARRIOR MOM OF 2

THE WARRIOR MOM HANDBOOK

CHAPTER 2

I remember the second day of boot camp after I joined the Air Force. Our leaders marched us across the base to a building. We entered and we proceeded through stations. At each station, we received an article of clothing that would become our daily wardrobe: socks, camouflage pants, brown undershirts, camouflage overshirts, a belt, a camouflage hat, and a jacket. When we arrived at the final station, a man yelled, "What shoe size?" Once you stated your shoe size, he plopped a pair of black leather boots on top of your nose-level stack, and then he said, "Move on!" The articles of clothing made us look like soldiers. The belt's role in all of this was simple, to keep the pants in place. If you research the belt in the Bible, you will find that it is frequently referred to as a simple article of clothing:

Exodus 12:11 (In reference to the Passover) *This is how you are to eat it: with your cloak tucked into your belt, your sandals on your feet and your staff in your hand. Eat it in haste; it is the Lord's Passover.*

I Kings 18:46 (Elijah on Mount Carmel — after a dare to the prophets of Baal. Their God did not show up, but the Lord — the God almighty, the God of Jacob did show up) *The power of the Lord came upon Elijah and, tucking his cloak into his belt, he ran ahead of Ahab all the way to Jezreel.*

II Kings 4:29 (The Shunammite's son restored to life; Elisha said to Gehazi) *Tuck your cloak into your belt, take my staff in your hand and run. If you meet anyone, do not greet him and if anyone greets you, do not answer. Lay my staff on the boy's face.*

II Kings 9:1-3 (Jehu anointed King of Israel; the prophet Elisha summoned a man from the company of the prophets and said to him) *Tuck your cloak into your belt, take this flask of oil with you and go to Ramoth Gilead. When you get there, look for Jehu son of Jehoshaphat, the son of Nimshi. Go to him, get him away from his companions and take him into the inner room. Then take the flask and pour the oil on his head and declare, "This is what the LORD says: I anoint you king over Israel." Then open the door and run; don't delay!*

Thus far, a belt in the Bible was used just as we use it. However, our clothes are not as cumbersome as their cloaks were. They were constantly grabbing hold of their cloaks and tucking them into their belts before they ran. In all these passages, the people needed to hurry up and get going. For me at boot camp, my belt kept my camouflage pants in place while I marched and/or ran laps. A belt was then and it is now just a belt. But don't you love how God takes ordinary objects and explains deeper meaning?

Isaiah 11:5 *Righteousness will be his belt and faithfulness the sash around his waist.*

Let's employ Webster to gain a deeper understanding of righteousness.

Righteousness: acting or being in accordance with what is just, honorable, free from guilt or wrong.

This leads into explaining how the belt is used in the following passage:

Ephesians 6:14 *Stand firm then, with the belt of truth buckled around your waist.*

What holds things in place is the truth! For the people in the Bible, and for me at boot camp, the belt held things in place as we marched or raced off to carry out our orders. In the spiritual realm, the truth holds you in place. Notice that it says, *"Stand firm then, with the belt of truth buckled around your waist."* Stand firm? Why do you need to stand firm? What is coming against you that would cause you to be weak? What is opposite of the truth? Lies. Who is the father of lies? The enemy. John 8:44 reads, *"When he lies, he speaks his native language, for he is a liar and the father of lies."* What kind of lies? Remember those things you listed earlier with which you may be struggling? Those things will be used against you. Lies of doubt will come to you. Lies about who you are, what your purpose is, and lies about not being forgiven. You name it: lies will come.

Below is a list of some lies that I have been hearing:
"You'll never amount to anything."
"You are crazy. You don't hear from God."
"You've screwed up so many times. Things will never work out for you."
"You are a bad mother."
"Your husband will leave you."
"You are ugly."
"You will always struggle with your weight."
"You'll be all alone."
"If you try, you will fail."
"_____ is jealous of you, and they hate you."
"_____ doesn't love you anyway."
"Who are you that you matter to God anyway?"
"You are just an idiot."
"You should feel so guilty over that last mess-up that you should never forgive yourself and move on."
"You shouldn't reach out to other women. They'll just hurt you like they did before."
"The ladies in the church do worse things than ladies who don't even go to church."
"Don't spend the energy. It won't be worth it."
"Stay isolated and by yourself. You'll feel better."
"Just quit. You'll never make it anyway."

Can you think of some lies that you have heard? I know that each woman has unique lies that she's been hearing for years. Anne, one of the original Warrior Moms, said that it's like listening to a broken CD over and over again. Nicole C. Mullens sings a song called *Brainwash* that talks about this topic. One of the original Warrior Moms, Brenda, sent it to me one morning, and I listened to it while I edited this handbook and drank my coffee. It's an awesome song! You've listened to the same lies for so many years that you actually think it's truth. And now, you actually say them to yourself. What happens is this: the enemy whispers them to you until you start to whisper them to yourself for him. Then, he is freed up to bug someone else because he's got you defeating yourself with the original lies that he gave you. And you wake each day and play the same CD over and over again! Wake up! Wake up. It's crucial that you wake up. Snap out of the trance. Throw that old CD away! Lies keep you in bondage to defeat and doubt, but *"the truth will set you free!"* (John 8:32)

SKIT
Lucy and Ethel

Lucy: A woman who realizes she's been listening to a recording of lies, and who shares the good news with her neighbor
Ethel: The neighbor who is informed of the good news
Narrator: A woman who provides the voice of insight and directions for the skit

[BEGIN SCENE]

Narrator: Do you remember the movie *Groundhog Day*? That guy woke up each day and stepped in the same puddle time after time after time. Picture women all around the globe waking up each day. They reach over, turn off their alarm clocks, grab the same CD out of their top dresser drawers, walk to the kitchen, make coffee, and put in the disc. As they do dishes, make lunches, and get kids ready for the day, they play the CD and listen to the same old lies over and over again.

And, more importantly, they listen to the CD in isolation. And because they remain in isolation, they don't know that their neighbor, and her neighbor, and her neighbor are in their houses listening to the same disc of lies. Once one lady realizes that she's been in a trance listening to lies for years, she throws the old CD in the trash. As she pulls the trash to the curb for garbage pick-up day (and it really is garbage pick-up day because that broken CD will be picked up and dropped in a landfill where it belongs), she happens to look into her neighbor's kitchen window. She notices that her next door neighbor, Ethel, is putting a CD into the player and reaching for her . . .

Lucy: "Stop!"

Narrator: Lucy yells from the curb. She runs across her lawn, through Ethel's yard, up her porch and pounds hard three times on Ethel's door.

Lucy: [* knock on something hard "knock, knock, knock" and then say:] "Don't do it!"

Narrator: Lucy yells and pounds on Ethel's front door until she finally answers.

Ethel: "What in the world are you doing, Lucy?! You're in your pajamas!"

Lucy: "I saw you putting that CD into your CD player. Can I see it?"

Ethel: "Well, okay, I'll let you see my CD, but I don't know why you want to see my CD. Don't you have your own anyway?"

THE BELT OF TRUTH

Narrator: Ethel leaves Lucy standing on her front porch, goes to get her CD, and returns with it in her hand.

Lucy: "What does it say on the front of your CD?"

Ethel: Oh, it just says, [*say the following in a surprised voice] "Lies I've Come to Believe as Truth.'"

Narrator: Ethel stares at the CD. Her eyes are wide open, and her chin is on the ground. She's in shock from what she just read. It's as if she is reading the title for the first time.

Ethel: "What have I been listening to, Lucy?"

Lucy: "Don't feel bad. I was listening to the same CD at my house all these years too."

Ethel: "I'm throwing this thing away!"

Lucy: "Get your trash. We'll walk it to the curb together. It is trash day, after all!"

Ethel: "Trash day is right!"

Narrator: Ethel breaks the CD over her right knee and then heaves the pieces into the trash can. Upon leaving their trash at the curb, both ladies decide that they must tell the other ladies in the neighborhood to stop listening to their CDs as well.

Lucy: "You go to the right, and I'll go to the left."

Ethel: "Yeah, and we won't stop until every woman in every house throws out their CDs."

Narrator: After a second thought, Lucy says...

Lucy: "Actually, let's go to the first two houses together, and then once we have enough women, let's split up and go to the other houses in groups. We don't want to separate. We must stick together."

Ethel: "Good plan. This is huge, isn't it Lucy?! To think we've been listening to these CDs all these years, and we've been right next door to each other!"

Narrator: The ladies walk hand in hand in their pink slippers and robes across the grass to Sue's house. To Gina, picking up a bicycle from her lawn, it looked as if their pink robes were reflecting pink and brown patches of camouflage. She blinked and rubbed her eyes a few times. Lucy and Ethel grabbed hold of the belts on their robes and pulled them tight before they ran to Sue's front door. Suddenly, their belts seemed to have a glow about them.

A week later, a cat meowed and a dog barked as the newspaper boy threw the morning news upon driveways, landing with a thud [*stomp one time with your foot]. As newspapers were unrolled, eyes were opened to the headline for the day. A buzz and echo started. If you listen carefully, you can hear people murmuring as they read the headline aloud over their coffee, "Warrior Moms Uniting around the Globe. Old Eight-Tracks, Records, Tapes, and CDs Overfill Landfills in Record Numbers."

[END OF SCENE]

Warrior Moms Unite! ™

Luke 18:16-17 *"Let the little children come to me, and do not hinder them, for the kingdom of God belongs to such as these. I tell you the truth, anyone who will not receive the kingdom of God like a little child will never enter it."*

John 1:17 *For the law was given through Moses; grace and truth came through Jesus Christ.*

John 6:47 *"I tell you the truth; he who believes has everlasting life."*

John 13:19-20 *"I am telling you now before it happens, so that when it does happen you will believe that I am He. I tell you the truth, whoever accepts anyone I send accepts me; and whoever accepts me accepts the one who sent me."*

THE BELT OF TRUTH

FIELD EXERCISES

1. Just as I did earlier, list the lies that you have been hearing over and over again on your own CD.
   _____
   _____
   _____
   _____
   _____
   _____
   _____

2. Restate the lies in truth form. You might even have to write the exact opposite.
   _____
   _____
   _____
   _____
   _____
   _____
   _____

3. Now, find scripture for each truth that supports it. As you find the scripture, go back and write that scripture below each truthful statement. Example: My lie: "I can't do anything." Truth: "I am able." Scripture that supports the truth: Philippians 4:13 *"I can do everything through him who gives me strength."*

My lie: _____
Truth: _____
Scripture that supports the truth: _____

My lie: _____
Truth: _____
Scripture that supports the truth: _____

My lie: _____
Truth: _____
Scripture that supports the truth: _____

My lie: _____
Truth: _____
Scripture that supports the truth: _____

My lie: _____
Truth: _____
Scripture that supports the truth: _____

My lie: _____
Truth: _____
Scripture that supports the truth: _____

4. When you finish this assignment, begin to memorize your scripture verses.

Warrior Moms Unite! ™

www.WarriorMoms.net

CHAPTER 3

At one of our meetings, we began to discuss the ever-famous question. "Why?!" Here is an excerpt from an email that I sent to the class.

AN EMAIL

Hi Ladies: God gave me wonderful clarity about a few things regarding Warrior Moms and fruits of the Spirit:

Remember when I was talking about how in the military you don't ask, Why? Because in that split second of asking Why?, you just took a bullet? I also discuss this in my book entitled Do You Hear What I Hear? about how I told God, "Okay, I won't ask, 'Why is my son deaf?' but I'll ask, 'How do I go on from here and what do I do?'"

Well, love is the answer to the questions. Having love as the answer enables us not to be concerned with the Why? You might want to read that a few times. It's such a time and emotional saver.

Having love as the answer enables us not to be concerned with the Why!

If God had to first explain Why?, He and Jesus would still be sitting at their conference table in heaven and salvation would still be pending. If a commander in the Army had to explain Why? to the private, the mission would not get carried out. If a parent had to explain Why? to a 16 year old, he or she would have to sit there for four years just so the 16 year old could mature enough (literally the brain has to grow and make more connections) to even comprehend the parent's 30 minute explanation of Why? This is why parents just say, "Because I said so. You'll understand when you're older."

And such is the case with God and His soldiers. Don't waste your time with Why?, but instead ask what do I do? And how do I do it? Because the truth of the matter is that we are like the 16 year old to God, and we have to mature more, go through more, and be taught more. Our spiritual endurance has to be strengthened in order to understand a very detailed answer to the Why? And really, the long and the short of it is the answer is love anyway. Love. That's why God sent His son and love is why He asks us to do things that we feel are confusing and difficult. Love is the answer.

Galatians 5:22-26 *But the fruit of the Spirit is love, joy, peace, patience, kindness, goodness, faithfulness, gentleness and self-control. Against such things there is no law. Those who belong to Christ Jesus have crucified the sinful nature with its passions and desires. Since we live by the Spirit, let us keep in step with the Spirit. Let us not become conceited, provoking and envying each other.*

We've discussed that love is the answer to any Why? There is no need to waste time and energy there. In the time we waste with Why's, we or someone else we know might take a spiritual bullet; there's no time to waste.

THE FIRST FRUIT: LOVE

A VISUAL FOR YOU
More on Why

When I was in the Air Force, I shipped weapons and ammo to the Rangers in Desert Storm. I even loaded the Rangers themselves onto airplanes. So, if on one particular night I wasted precious time asking my commander questions like, "Why do I have to work at night? Why do I have to pull a double? Why do I have to load this ammo by myself?", and this resulted in being 75 minutes late loading the weapons and ammo, what might the result be? What if an already deployed Ranger who was awaiting his next shipment of resupply ammo got his shipment at 12:30 instead of 11:15? What if it just happened that he needed that ammo at 11:15 to save his life and the lives of those around him?

Such is the case in the spiritual realm. There are wars going on and things we must do even though we don't understand the Why's to them. The short answer to the Why? is love. The long answer to the Why? will be given to us on the other side of glory.

I Corinthians 13:8-12   *Love never fails. But when there are prophecies, they will cease; where there are tongues, they will be stilled; where there is knowledge, it will pass away. For we know in part and we prophesy in part, but when perfection comes, the imperfect disappears. When I was a child I talked like a child, I thought like a child, I reasoned like a child. When I became a man [or a Warrior Mom], I put childish ways behind me. Now we see but a poor reflection as in a mirror; then we shall see face to face. Now I know in part; then I shall know fully; even as I am fully known.*

In short, God will give us the long version, but for now we take the answer to our Why? as love. Soldiers go to war and fight for love of country. We've all heard that before. We must also know that while many young men and women enlisted in the military after September 11 out of anger over what the terrorists did to us, it was love — not anger — that fueled their strength during battle. Anger does provide a quick burst of energy, but love provides the lasting energy needed to endure.

Love is the answer.

I Corinthians 16:13-14   *Be on guard; stand firm in the faith; be men of courage; be strong. Do everything in love.*

We must do things in love not anger.

Romans 12:17-21 *Do not repay anyone evil for evil. Be careful to do what is right in the eyes of everybody. If it is possible, as far as it depends on you, live in peace with everyone. Do not take revenge, my friends, but leave room for God's wrath, for it is written: "It is mine to revenge; I will repay," says the Lord. On the contrary: "If your enemy is hungry, feed him; if he is thirsty, give him something to drink. In doing so, you will heap burning coals on his head." Do not overcome evil by evil, but overcome evil with good.*

Now, I'm not going to go into complicated issues about whether we should or shouldn't have gone to war after 9/11. I do know that when you are spiritually attacked by the enemy, you must defend yourself with the Word of God. My point in bringing up 9/11 and the fact that many young men and women enlisted in the military afterwards is this: initially they may have joined in anger, for revenge, in fear, in courage, in love, in hate — whatever their reasons were. Ultimately, the one reason that sustained them through what was awaiting them in war was love. Love allows women to lift cars off of their children after accidents. Love enables a husband to stand by his wife's bed as she dies. Love allows parents to be tough when their children need it. Love causes nations and people to rise up. Love kept Jesus on that cross. *"Love covers a multitude of sin."* (I Peter 4:8)

I Corinthians 13:4-7 *Love is patient, love is kind. It does not envy, it does not boast, it is not proud. It is not rude, it is not self-seeking, it is not easily angered, it keeps no record of wrongs. Love does not delight in evil but rejoices with truth. It always protects, always trusts, always perseveres.*

In discussing love and the other fruits of the Spirit, we discovered that a Warrior Mom must be nourished with the fruit of the Spirit if she expects to endure through battles and wars. We also discovered that love is what holds the armor together. Without it, we are just warriors without a cause. Love gives the armor life and strength to persevere. This makes sense because "God is love." (I John 4:16) It makes sense then that love holds the armor together because God holds all things together. Colossians 1:17 states, "He is before all things, and in him all things hold together."

Ephesians 4:26 *In your anger do not sin. Do not let the sun go down while you are still angry, and do not give the devil a foothold.*

The key here is to learn how to differentiate between your anger and God's love. Unleashing your anger will add to the war, but unleashing God's love on the situation will cause peace to resonate throughout the land.

What gets in the way for you? Are you led by emotion and incited to your own self-righteous anger? How has that worked for you in the past? Yes, I got the same results. So, we have learned: *"Do not repay anyone evil for evil. Be careful to do what is right in the eyes of everybody. If it is possible, as far as it depends on you, live in peace with everyone. Do not take revenge, my friends, but leave room for God's wrath, for it is written: "It is mine to revenge; I will repay," says the Lord. On the contrary: "If your enemy is hungry, feed him; if he is thirsty, give him something to drink. In doing so, you will heap burning coals on his head."* (Romans 12:17-20)

THE FIRST FRUIT: LOVE

SKIT
The Tennis Match

Player 1: A teenager who starts a fight by delivering insults to her friend
Player 2: A teenager who receives insults and responds with additional insults
Narrator: A woman who provides the voice of insight and directions for the skit

[BEGIN SCENE]

Narrator:	Two teenage girls are playing tennis. One girl gets mad and begins to hurl an insult, along with the tennis ball, across the net.
Player 1:	"You're awful. You'll never win!"
Player 2:	"Oh yeah, well, you're awful, and you've always been awful!"
Player 1:	"Well, I've thought you stunk since we were five!"
Player 2:	"Oh yeah, well, your hair looks ridiculous that way, and I've always wanted to tell you that!"
Player 1:	"Oh yeah, well, about those jeans that you asked me if you look good in. You actually don't!"
Player 2:	"Oh yeah, well, your prom dress was the ugliest color this side of Mars! In fact, it looked like the color of Mars!"
Player 1:	"Well, your Mama . . ."

[END OF SCENE]

Okay, while this is a silly example, it's exactly what happens in the real world. When an argument starts, whether it's between two 16 year old girls on a tennis court or not, it still resembles a tennis match with each player trying to retaliate with a more disturbing insult than the one they just received.

What does God mean when he talks about being nice and putting burning coals on someone's head?

Proverbs 25:22 *If your enemy is hungry, give him food to eat; if he is thirsty, give him water to drink. In doing this, you will heap burning coals on his head, and the Lord will reward you.*

(And, by the way, ultimately, the coals are being put on the enemy's head. Remember, we do not battle against flesh and blood). Picture the same two girls:

SKIT
No Match

Player 1: A teenager who tries to start a fight by delivering insults to her friend
Player 2: A teenager who receives insults and responds in love

[BEGIN SCENE]

Player 1: "You're awful, you'll never win!"

Player 2: "Oh." [silence]

Player 1: "I've thought you stunk since we were five!"

Player 2: "I've always loved and valued your friendship."

Player 1: "Oh yeah, well, about those jeans that you asked me if you look good in. You actually don't!"

Player 2: [silence]

Player 1: "Well, your Mama . . ."

Player 2: "My Father loves you so much. He sent His only begotten son to die so that whomever might believe in Him shall not perish but have everlasting life." (John 3:16).

Player 1: "What are you doing?! I'm trying to have a fight with you and you won't participate?!"

[END OF SCENE]

Case in point—people can't continue to play tennis with you if you don't return the ball. I read somewhere once, "Never argue too long with an idiot, people will begin to wonder who the idiot is." The spiritually smart woman responds in peace."

II Timothy 2:23-26 *Don't have anything to do with foolish and stupid arguments, because you know they produce quarrels. And the Lord's servant must not quarrel; instead, he must be kind to everyone, able to teach, not resentful. Those who oppose him he must gently instruct, in the hope that God will grant them repentance leading them to the knowledge of the truth, and that they will come to their senses and escape the trap of the devil, who has taken them captive to do his will.*

Titus 2:6-8 *Similarly, encourage the young men to be self-controlled. In everything set them an example by doing what is good. In your teaching show integrity, seriousness and soundness of speech that cannot be condemned, so that those who oppose you may be ashamed because they have nothing bad to say about us."*

Eventually, the person who has been hurling insults at you will get tired, bored or both and will stop. It's difficult to refrain from responding, but once you've done it the first time, it will be easier the next time, and the time after that, and the time after that. You'll be amazed at the results! And don't worry if you struggle with this one. Fortunately and unfortunately, in this life, you'll get plenty of opportunities to improve this skill.

THE FIRST FRUIT: LOVE

I Corinthians 16:13-14 *Be on guard; stand firm in the faith; be men of courage; be strong. Do everything in love.*

Unleashing your anger will add to the war, but unleashing God's love on the situation will cause peace to resonate throughout the land. We must do things in love, not anger.

A VISUAL FOR YOU
An Illustration of a Battle

I was upset with my husband, and it had gone on for about four and a half weeks. I was tired. I was feeling hurt, even angry, ready to fight about it all. But, I knew not to give into all that. So, I prayed. I prayed, and prayed, and prayed. But, I was still hurt. My husband hurt my feelings. It seemed he wasn't listening. He kept interrupting me in the middle of my sentences, saying, "Oh! ...", remembering something he had forgotten about his day — to bring something home, to drop the students' grades in the grading system at his school. He seemed to be more interested in other things than me. He'd been falling asleep on the couch for three weeks now. I couldn't really blame him; after all, I was up late studying in the den, but still, I felt hurt and angry, like he wasn't engaged. To me, he wasn't listening or helping me. It seemed like I was doing it all! I felt like I was doing everything around the house while he did whatever, which included watching football and the news. I had had it!

I asked God for help. I didn't want to get into a big fight. We didn't fight anyway. We've been married almost 17 years, and we quit fighting years ago. Now we actually talk like adults about things. So why hadn't I talked with him? I was worried that my issues might have more to do with me than him.

God taught me a while ago to look at myself before I accuse other people of junk. I had been spending a lot of time with God asking Him to do a new work in me, to reveal things of my heart to me. I didn't want to rush ahead of God. Lord knows I had done that enough in my life, and I've suffered enough of those messy consequences. I was really trying to wait on God. And, God was working on me, so I was trying to be patient with my husband because I knew God just might probably need to do something in me first. This might be all about my own issues anyway.

In fact, just recently, God told me that I have a tendency to get mad and defensive when I'm scared, that I almost turn into a bit of a bully. That hit home. He was right. In fact, a couple of years ago, I realized that my tough exterior was comprised of a serious look on my face, and always walking with intense purpose, with a vertical wrinkle in between my eyebrows. This vertical wrinkle was from years of looking tough to keep other people away. I knew it originated from my childhood, that awful place of alcoholics and physical abuse. It made sense.

It was a defense mechanism, but I was an adult now. I was a child of God now! I shouldn't have to have a face like that, to walk like that to stay safe anymore. So a few years ago, I asked God to help me. I started pulling my face back—the muscles anyway. I started making a conscious effort to not have that intense wrinkle in between my eyebrows. I started walking more calmly, not so fast. I started lowering my shoulders and stopped looking like I was about to tackle someone like a football player.

I had improved. So when God told me that I have a tendency to get defensive when I'm scared, well, that wasn't a shocker. I guess I had gotten better at the physical expression of being calmer, but I still had work to do on internal peace. I was thinking about what He said when I heard His voice. *"And you do it to Me too."*

I looked up to the ceiling in shock. "What?!" "Oh, my goodness, I do, don't I?" I apologized to God because it would make sense that if I do it in general, I do it to God too. God was so nice to me about it. He just let me know that this was an area that He wanted me to work on; it would lead to more peace and a keener ability to listen more acutely to Him in the Spirit. After all, I had asked Him to reveal things within my heart that needed work. I was reminded of how God disciplines us, how He teaches us, how He doesn't do it with condemnation and guilt, but He kindly lets us know, "Let's work on this area, child," and He still makes you feel extremely loved in the process.

God's gentle guidance reminded me of a conversation I had with Faith, my daughter, recently. She is a peer leader in her middle school, which means she spends one class period each day with her community counselor. Some days she goes to another class and helps other kids, other days she has classes with her school counselor about improving her communication skills, setting examples, leading, teaching, all kinds of cool things like that. They went to a leadership conference recently, where they received t-shirts with a big eagle on the front and *Professional Role Model* on the back.

She was wearing her t-shirt one day, sitting at lunch, and a girl at her table said, "Just look at Casie! She's getting so fat!"

Another girl replied, "She is!"

"Well, that's not nice to say, especially behind her back like that. How would you like it if I was talking about you like that behind your back?" Faith asked.

"Well, I'm not fat, so you wouldn't," the girl responded.

Faith countered, "Well, still, it's not nice to do that, so until you're perfect, why don't you lay off other people."

"Well, excuse me, Faith, if I'm not a *professional role model* like you!"

"You don't have to be a professional role model to be a nice person," Faith argued.

Long story short, it went back and forth for a while, and Faith kept on returning the comments to the girl, until the girl stopped.

Faith told me about it on the way to the phone store one night. I told her I was proud of her for sticking up for Casie. Then after we left the store on the way home, I talked with her about stopping after two comments next time. We discussed how it was good to stand up for someone else, but she basically humiliated the girl who messed up.

Faith said, "Good, she deserved it too!"

We continued to talk about how God teaches us things and if He does it in a nice, not humiliating way, then He wants us to do the same when we teach other people things. It's not good to kick a horse 20 times to get your point across. In fact, it's never well received when we do things that way; it incites anger and resentment rather than teaches a lesson that will bring positive change.

THE FIRST FRUIT: LOVE

We talked about how saying something nice about Casie, then changing the subject (not feeding the hatred), may work better next time. People learn by our example more than they do from our words, anyway. I have learned that it's better to try to lead by example and pray in the Word rather than spew off things from my mouth and slay dragons all by myself. I usually end up with the sword in my side (or my back) when I do it that way.

Why did I just tell you that story? Well, funny how our own lessons end up on our own heads sometimes, which brings me back to my feeling hurt about my husband. I did good one day. I was obedient to God and I got the reward, but another day I was not. Let me first start by talking about how I was good. I feel compelled to tell you the good so you'll understand my mess-up.

I was praying about what I might need to work on. God revealed to me that I get defensive when I'm scared and that I do it to Him, too. I was still struggling with my husband not really helping me out. Usually, he mows the lawn, and I do the grocery shopping. It was fall and the grass was pretty much dead. He hadn't had to mow the lawn for about three weeks, but my stuff—groceries, house, the kids, errands — hadn't let up at all. I usually don't keep track of who does what. It generally balances itself out. But when his mowing chores petered out and he hadn't shared in cooking dinner for six nights, I felt resentment build in my gut like a slow, festering boil.

On top of that, he was stressed and exhausted from working on his Master's degree and asked me to take over the checkbook responsibilities. I was trying to pick up the slack, and I was about worn out, mad, hurt, just done! But, still, I was trying to be obedient to God. I prayed and prayed about it because I felt that if I discussed it with my husband, I would flip out and forget all my communication and spiritual skills.

One Sunday afternoon, I was working on schoolwork for my Doctorate in Clinical Psychology. The program was demanding, exhausting, and much bigger than me, but not bigger than God. Brian was on the couch, alternately watching football and napping. I had asked him a month earlier to help me figure out how to hook up our new printer so our laptops would print to it. I wasn't sure if we routed it through the DSL line or if we should get a cable. That was his department.

We both needed the printer. I especially needed to print out my psychological reports to be able to proof them before I emailed them to the psychologists I was interning under and to my professors for a grade. In fact, I had already turned in six reports that I had to proof on the computer screen, which is next to impossible for me! I still had to go to the grocery store, finish two reports, and take care of other chores. Fuming, I felt like yelling at Brian, telling him to get off the couch, turn off the TV, and go to the store for me! But, I knew that wouldn't prove successful. Instead I prayed, "Please God! Help me here! Please just tell my husband to go to the store and get that cable for us — he needs it also — but I really need help here. Please just impress upon his heart that he needs to go get it."

I prayed for 30 minutes on my knees in the den. Everyone thought I was writing a report, but I was in there petitioning to God over a printer cable! This was serious here. It was like the printer cable was life or death for me as far as my sanity, my marriage, my health! Have you ever been there? It's like one thing will make such a huge difference to your life and heart that you pray to God that He'll work it out for you, and then you can breathe.

Eventually I stopped praying, and I got busy with schoolwork. About two hours later, Brian walked down the hall, tapped on the door and said, "Well, after I clean up the lunch dishes, I guess I'll go get that computer cable."

Remember, I hadn't mentioned the thing in 30 days! It was all I could do to not start running around saying, "Praise Jesus, praise Jesus, praise Jesus!" I did it in my head and said, "Oh, thank you so much! That will really help me today, and it'll help you also. Don't you have to print an article out and review it for class?"

"Yep, I do, so I'll go get it in a little bit here."

Can I get an Amen?! Raise your hand if you've been there?! God is so amazing!

That was my "good, obedient thing." I waited on God and received the blessing. I held myself back in the physical, put the hurt and anger aside, and asked God to work it out, and He did. But, I still had issues with being hurt and feeling like Brian wasn't listening. I was talking one night and he did that "Oh!" thing again. I stopped talking, and he didn't even realize that I never finished what I was saying. I went down the hall to my bedroom, big tears streaking down my cheeks.

I prayed about what to do, telling God that I really wanted to talk with Brian, that I needed to tell him that he'd been hurting my feelings, and that I really wanted him to listen to me and let me finish a sentence. God didn't say anything. Since I had gone running earlier, I decided to take a shower. I kept talking to God about my dilemma in the shower. When I was finished and walking through my bedroom door, I felt like God said, *"Wait until tomorrow."* I didn't really listen though because, frankly, I didn't want to obey what He said. I was hurt and had had enough. I needed to talk, and since I didn't want to listen to what God might have said to me, I decided that I would have a little talk with my husband. I could do that, just express my thoughts and stay cool. It didn't have to be a fight. I lifted my head and marched down the hall, even though I felt deep down I should wait.

I spoke to Brian, and although everything I said was true, it made him feel horrible. He didn't even argue with me. It was as if he knew he hadn't been paying attention or doing anything for me for a while. But I felt the conversation was a disaster because I made myself feel better by making him feel bad.

My selfish, disobedient action created a palpable yuck in the air. I could feel it and soon knew it was affecting our household. As I walked down the hall, I heard Brian and our son, Jacob, begin to argue. Brian was provoking Jacob through an old behavior of teasing and disciplining at the same time; it made me furious. He'd only done it a handful of times in the last 13 years. It's been one of those parenting issues that we've argued over, not a huge one, but one that Brian has worked on.

When I heard him speak to our son that way, I felt rage boiling in my veins. It was all I could do to close the office door without slamming it so I could pray. In the silence of the office, I heard God say, *"You unleashed it."*

"I did, didn't I?" I replied. "Now what?! I was rude and disrespectful to my husband in the first place. Oh, my God, help me, help us. How do we get this yuck out of our home tonight?!"

Instantly, I got on my knees and prayed and cast it out. I stood up and quoted scripture. I moved my arms around and commanded that this evil leave my home in the name of Jesus Christ! Breaking into a sweat, I opened the den door, walked down the hall and sat down to talk with my husband and son. I changed the subject and soon the tone transformed; the air wasn't thick anymore. I could feel that the yuck had left. Jesus worked through me to bring peace back! But I had to wrestle with my flesh. Believe me, I wanted to get in a

THE FIRST FRUIT: LOVE

big fight with Brian over it. But I had to let God fight the battle for me because I knew that if I gave in to my desire for confrontation, I'd get a war—a big, physical, bloody war—and who wins in that type of situation? The enemy! Thankfully, God helped me wrestle the flesh (emotional yuck) off of me. Afterwards, He was able to work through me in the spiritual realm and restore peace to my "homeland."

The next morning, I got up to make lunches for my family. I make Brian various kinds of sandwiches and pack great stuff like special cheeses, different kinds of meat, and different types of chips. On Sundays, I pick meats that I will use that week, and I alternate the cheeses: Swiss, provolone, etc. And I always write a note on everyone's napkin. For my husband, I try to come up with a new saying each time, which takes some creativity. I write notes like, "I love you more every day," "You make my heart smile," "You amaze me," "Thank you for being my prince," "I love your smile," "Your eyes are sooo kind," etc. Okay, stop gagging!

God told me to do this about six years ago. I didn't want to at first because I thought Brian didn't deserve the sandwich (that's another story written in a different book), but I told God I would make the lunch for Him, but only because I was being obedient, not because I wanted to. So, for six years, I have been making the sandwiches. At first it started out as me doing it for God, *not for my husband*, but eventually God taught me a lot about serving others, even when we feel they don't deserve it — especially when we feel they don't deserve it. And if we do that, God will work it together *for the good of those who love him* (Romans 8:28). And God has too! My heart and my marriage changed for the better as a result. Both Brian and I developed more of a servant-like heart. From my example of doing for him, my husband began to do more for me. It melted anger and resentment, and it revolutionized our house! I'm serious! A sandwich did all that. Actually, God did it through a sandwich (through an act of service).

What's my point? Well, I got up the next day to make sandwiches and under my note on yesterday's napkin was a note from my husband telling me, "You're amazing! I love you! Thanks for all you do!" Under that was another note in a different color that said, "PS, I wrote that note (with an arrow) during lunch yesterday."

When I read the note, I knew that God had said, *"Wait until tomorrow."* Had I waited, I would have realized that God was already impressing upon my husband that I needed a note, and He had already put it on my husband's heart to write me one — yesterday! And God told me to wait because unknown to me, there was a note waiting for me on an old napkin with mustard on it from yesterday's lunch inside my husband's lunch box! Then it hit me. I had done to my husband exactly what I told Faith not to do: kick a dead horse to make your point.

No wonder it wasn't well received! I wasn't supposed to do that. I was supposed to wait on God, and I hadn't. I was so humbled! I felt like a heel.

Brian walked into the kitchen about that time. While holding yesterday's mustard-smeared napkin, I said, "Well, I guess I was supposed to wait 'til today to talk with you, and then I wouldn't have even talked to you about all that because I had a note waiting for me."

"No, you're right. In fact, I was thinking that I hadn't been giving you much attention lately, and that I hadn't written you a note in a long time. So I wrote you one during lunch yesterday."

"I'm sorry," I said.

"No, I'm sorry that you've been feeling bad and that I hurt your feelings," he said.

We hugged, but deep down I knew that I had been disobedient to God, which had in turn caused more harm to my husband's heart than help to him and our marriage. I apologized to God, too! Gees, I felt so bad.

When everyone left for school, I poured myself a cup of coffee and talked with God about all of this, how it all came full circle on my head. I reflected back on how I was blessed when I was obedient and how I unleashed evil in my home when I was not. *"In your anger do not sin. Do not let the sun go down while you are still angry, and do not give the devil a foothold."* (Ephesians 4:26-27) And that's exactly what I had done. When God said, *"You unleashed it,"* I knew exactly what He meant. That little foothold is all the enemy needs to feed upon the flesh and try to devour us.

In Job, when God asks Satan where he's been, Satan replies, *"From roaming the earth and going back and forth in it."* (Job 6-7) And I Peter 5:6-10 reads, *"Humble yourselves, therefore, under God's mighty hand, that he may lift you up in due time. Cast all your anxiety on him because he cares for you. Be self-controlled and alert. Your enemy the devil prowls around like a roaring lion looking for someone to devour. Resist him, standing firm in the faith, because you know that your brothers throughout the world are undergoing the same kind of sufferings. And the God of all grace, who called you to his eternal glory in Christ, after you have suffered a little while, will himself restore you and make you strong, firm and steadfast. To him be the power forever and ever. Amen."*

This story is not just about some mom across the country in Georgia with little, silly hurts and events. It's not June and not Ward in another town. This is about the battles that go on within our homelands. It's about how if we are not alert, we will fall into the traps that the enemy sets for us. They are little traps; tiny little traps. I believe that the enemy walks to and fro and sets up one a day, maybe one every other day in our lives. Because we don't notice them, we are vulnerable. He constantly incites us to fall for them, and when we are weakened from all the previous traps, he pounces on us! The enemy brings in more forces, more evil, and kicks us while we are down. He kicks and kicks and jumps on us and spits in our spiritual faces through the physical, silly, little situations. Of course, if we give him a foothold, we unleash it all!

Do you see the power of this?! We've cracked the code! We have cracked it wide open. We must, therefore, be alert about our spiritual blind spots and ask God to reveal those blind spots to us, those pesky, little, fleshly emotional traps.

I saw something in my mind one night when I was discussing all of this with Brenn, another Warrior Mom. We were on fire about this revelation. I saw myself when I gave in and gave the enemy a foothold by not being obedient. I saw an image as if I had actually created more physical flesh for the enemy to gorge himself upon. Now stick with me. This is a bit complicated and confusing — it was to me anyway — but allow your minds to open up and think without limits. What I saw was that the flesh that he actually gorges himself upon is really spiritual flesh created through physical circumstances. Think about that for a moment and then move on.

THE FIRST FRUIT: LOVE

The enemy has to convert our physical junk because he is a spiritual being. So he has to take physical circumstances like our physical weaknesses and incite us. He puts out the bait and then when we fall for it, we fall into the trap. Then and only then does he have the power to create a spiritual feast out of us!

It's as if our disobedience and our acts of giving him a foothold create the meal for him, and the more we do it, the bigger his meal becomes and the greater our destruction. So, if we give into it, it's like he devours us. We actually offered the meal up to him — our own selves — based upon not being obedient, and we gave him the fork, knife and salt and pepper! An important point to make is that most of the time we don't mean to do it. We were hurt after all; our hearts were broken. We did it out of ignorance, but we still end up with A.1.® Steak Sauce all over us as we became a lion's meal!

What I want to pray for, then, is that God would speak so loudly to us in the spiritual, that He would give us so much strength in the spiritual, that we would be aware of the seemingly little pesky physical issues of our days, of our lives, and of our homes. I pray that we are alert to this war against our homes, against our marriages, and against our children.

"Finally, be strong in the Lord and in his mighty power. Put on the full armor of God so that you can take your stand against the devil's schemes. For our struggle is not against flesh and blood, but against the rulers, against the authorities against the powers of this dark world and against the spiritual forces of evil in the heavenly realms. Therefore put on the full armor of God, so that when the day of evil comes, you may be able to stand your ground, and after you have done everything, to stand. Stand firm then, with the belt of truth buckled around your waist, with the breastplate of righteousness in place, and with your feet fitted with the readiness that comes from the gospel of peace. In addition to all this, take up the shield of faith, with which you can extinguish all the flaming arrows of the evil one. Take the helmet of salvation and the sword of the Spirit, which is the word of God. And pray in the Spirit on all occasions with all kinds of prayers and requests. With this in mind, be alert and always keep on praying for all the saints." (Ephesians 6:10-19) When God taps you on the shoulder and tells you to wait, wait. Listen to God.

Here's one more small, but huge revelation about God telling me that I have a tendency to get defensive when I'm scared. During the episode described above, my hurt feelings were really about me being scared about many things in our lives. For one, I was scared because my husband was exhausted, which made me feel fearful and alone, which in turn caused me to get defensive! In my defensiveness, I have a tendency to become angry. Anger is so much easier than dealing with the issues underneath the anger. So, really, a lot of this started a while ago, without my awareness. In the future, I'll talk with Brian about both of our fears and about forming more of a united front together. But I'll be praying about it and letting God lead me through it. I have realized that God is so nice to me when He corrects me and teaches me, and I need to be the same way with others. *"Some of you have become arrogant, as if I were not coming to you. But I will come to you very soon, if the Lord is willing, and then I will find out not only how these arrogant people are talking, but what power they have. For the kingdom of God is not a matter of talk but of power. What do you prefer? Shall I come to you with a whip, or in love with a gentle spirit?"* (I Corinthians 4:18-21)

A VISUAL FOR YOU
A Slow Fade

Sometimes my children enjoy eating lunch at the coffee table. Jacob is 11 and his body is small so he has plenty of room. Faith, on the other hand, will be 15 this month and her legs are longer than my husband's and mine. Needless to say, she doesn't fit so well in between the loveseat and the coffee table. If Jacob gets there first, he's already nicely placed and settled, eating his lunch. Then, Faith shows up and has to maneuver herself into position. She usually looks like she's playing a game of *Twister* while she gets herself situated.

The other day, I was sitting on the couch watching Faith. She did something different this time and I tried not to laugh. Jacob was already settled and eating at the coffee table which was further out from the loveseat than it usually is. This meant that Faith had more room, but it also meant that when she sat down and began to eat, the coffee table was actually too far away.

In the past, Faith would reach out and quickly jerk the coffee table toward her to which Jacob would yell, "Hey Faith!" This time, I watched Faith reach out and slowly, slowly, slowly, ever so gradually start to pull the coffee table toward her. I looked at Jacob. He didn't even notice. He was eating his food and drinking his milk, and didn't even realize that the table was being moved at a snail's pace. Sure, it took a while, but when Faith quit moving the table, it was perfectly placed in front of her so that she could comfortably lean on the back of the loveseat and eat her meal.

Now, the funny thing was that the coffee table was completely diagonal at this point, but Jacob didn't even notice. I saw Faith smirk with satisfaction as she took her first bite of food. I tried not to laugh. I thought it was mighty clever of her. She altered the placement of the coffee table without Jacob even noticing. She just had to be cautious and patient while she gradually moved the coffee table into position.

Not that I was super impressed with her tactic, but I was trying not to laugh out loud at what I had just witnessed. God said, "*See that, Kristina?*" Immediately, I knew what He meant. In regard to Warriors Moms and our enemy, the enemy moves ever so slowly, gradually and patiently moving things in our lives, setting little traps, pulling us away from the Word, day by day to the point where we don't even notice.

All of a sudden, one day, we wake up and we wonder what has happened to our faith, our energy, our passion for life, our hope, our friends, our community, our home lives, ourselves, our hearts, our sanity! Truth is we have experienced a slow fade of a gradual decrease in our faith. It made sense at the time - "We didn't have time for the Word, for exercise, to talk with and/or pray with a friend because (sure, we had good reasons), our business required us to be there more than we felt was a healthy balance, a boss demanded that we compromise, our child had a doctor's appointment, our spouse needed something at the store, our best friend who always calls with a crisis kept calling and we just had to respond, our kids needed help with homework, we had to run errands, every second of our free time was spent, etc., etc., etc.

And so we find ourselves in a "bad place" of thinking that church is lame because it just doesn't "do anything" for us anymore and we think the problem is with everyone else. We find ourselves a little bitter, resentful, and irritated with Christians who say, "Praise God!" like they really mean it. And sure, we are reminded of the

THE FIRST FRUIT: LOVE

people in the church who are actually hypocritical. So we think we are justified at judging everyone who praises God because they irritate the stew out of us. Truth is, there are people who say, "Praise God!" because they mean it, and there are people who say, "Praise God!" just to look good, but that's not what is really bothering us. Even Paul talked about people who preached Jesus Christ out of integrity and people who preached Jesus Christ out of selfish ambition (Philippians 1:17), and the two types of people will always exist.

Philippians 1:15-18   *It is true that some preach Christ out of envy and rivalry, but others out of goodwill. The latter do so in love, knowing that I am put here for the defense of the gospel. The former preach Christ out of selfish ambition, not sincerely, supposing that they can stir up trouble for meanwhile I am in chains. But what does it matter? The important thing is that in every way, whether from false motives or true, Christ is preached. And because of this I will rejoice.*

What is truly bothering us is that we want to be the type of person who says, "Praise God!" out of a genuine, authentic, real relationship with Jesus Christ (like Paul in chains), and somehow we feel that we've lost the ability to do so. Paul praised God whether well fed or hungry, whether in chains or free because he learned the secret of being content in all things.

Philippians 4: 4-13   *Rejoice in the Lord always. I will say it again: Rejoice! Let your gentleness be evident to all. The Lord is near. Do not be anxious about anything, but in everything, by prayer and petition, with thanksgiving, present your requests to God. And the peace of God, which transcends all understanding, will guard your hearts and your minds in Christ Jesus. Finally, brothers, whatever is true, whatever is noble, whatever is right, whatever is pure, whatever is lovely, whatever is admirable – if anything is excellent or praiseworthy – think about such things. Whatever you have learned or received or heard from me, or seen in me – put into practice. And the God of peace will be with you. I rejoice greatly in the Lord that at last you have renewed your concern for me. Indeed, you have been concerned, but you had no opportunity to show it. I am not saying this because I am in need, for I have learned to be content whatever the circumstances. I know what it is to be in need, and I know what it is to have plenty. I have learned the secret of being content in any and every situation, whether well fed or hungry, whether living in plenty or in want. I can do everything through him who gives me strength.*

And THAT, my fellow Warrior is what we want to have – the kind of passion and genuine relationship with Jesus Christ that Paul had, but somehow the banquet table of God's will gets slowly, ever so gradually moved. The enemy alters our focus from Christ without us even noticing. Sure, he had to be cautious and patient while he gradually shifted our focus so that he could attack us better. If he did a quick jerk, he would have been found out immediately. It would have been so obvious that even if you were sleeping it would have jolted you to attention and you would have said, "Aha, game over!" That would have been too simple. Remember, the enemy is the Father of Lies. If he acted in obvious ways, you would be able to stand firm in your steadfast position of praise and alertness without much effort. One thing is for sure, being a Warrior Mom always takes effort.

I hope this visual encourages you to find yourself consistently in the Word, consistently in prayer, and consistently in community with other believers. And may you find yourself truly living the life that is truly life!

John 10:10   *The thief comes only to steal and kill and destroy; I have come that they may have life, and have it to the full.*

 **FIELD EXERCISES**

1. How do you respond when you become angry? What do you say and/or do?
   _____
   _____

2. What have been some of the outcomes in situations when you responded in anger?
   _____
   _____

3. What do you appreciate about God?
   _____
   _____

4. Find a favorite verse in the Bible regarding God's love for you. Write it below and work to memorize it.
   _____
   _____

5. Look up 1 John 4:16 and write it here:
   _____
   _____

6. Now, look up 1 Corinthians 13:4-13. Since you know that God is love, read it and replace the word "God" with "love". I can see why God listed love as the first fruit.

7. Describe the main lesson you learned from this chapter.
   _____
   _____

8. When I was irritated with my husband regarding all the "things he wasn't doing," God asked me to make a list of all the things that he does that I never have to think about. The list of things that he does for me (that I have taken for granted) was longer than my first list. If you aren't married, think of another relationship. Make a list of what that person does for you, things that you've unknowingly taken for granted.
   _____
   _____

Warrior Moms Unite! ™

Add 5 verses on LOVE!!!
David & Music

www.WarriorMoms.net

THE WARRIOR MOM HANDBOOK

CHAPTER 4

You have the breastplate of righteousness, a metal shell that protects your heart from being led entirely by feelings of emotion. It protects your back so that deceit cannot penetrate it and pierce your heart.

Let's look at references to the breastplate (piece) in the Bible.

Ephesians 6:14-15   *Stand firm then, with the belt of truth buckled around your waist, with the breastplate of righteousness in place, and with your feet fitted with the readiness that comes from the gospel of peace.*

Exodus 28:15-30   *"Fashion a breastpiece for making decisions – the work of a skilled craftsman. Make it like the ephod: of gold, and of blue, purple and scarlet yarn, and of finely twisted linen. It is to be square – a span long and a span wide – and folded double. Then mount four rows of precious stones on it. In the first row there shall be a ruby, a topaz and a beryl; in the second row a turquoise, a sapphire and an emerald; in the third row a jacinth, and agate and an amethyst; in the fourth row chrysolite, and onyx and jasper. Mount them in gold filigree settings. There are to be twelve stones, one of each of the names of the sons of Israel, each engraved like a seal with the name of one of the twelve tribes.*

"For the breastpiece make braided chains of pure gold, like a rope. Make two gold rings for it and fasten them to two corners of the breastpiece. Fasten the two gold chains to the rings at the corners of the breastpiece, and the other ends of the chains to the two settings, attaching them to the shoulder pieces of the ephod at the front. Make two gold rings and attach them to the other two corners of the breastpiece on the inside edge next to the ephod. Make two more gold rings and attach them to the bottom of the shoulder pieces on the front of the ephod, close to the seam just above the waistband of the ephod. The rings of the breastpiece are to be tied to the rings of the ephod with blue cord, connecting it to the waistband, so that the breastpiece will not swing out from the ephod.

"Whenever Aaron enters the Holy Place, he will bear the names of the sons of Israel over his heart on the breastpiece of decision as a continuing memorial before the Lord. Also put the Urim and the Thummim in the breastpiece, so they may be over Aaron's heart whenever he enters the presence of the Lord. Thus Aaron will always bear the means of making decisions for the Israelites over his heart before the Lord."

A number of questions arise. What is an ephod? What are the Urim and Thummim? An ephod is a type of shirt worn under the breastpiece. It is clearly defined in the following website: http://oce.catholic.com/index.php?title=Ephod and reads as this: Ephod: an oblong piece of cloth bound round the body under the arms reaching as far as the waist. Its material was fine-twisted linen embroidered with violet, purple, and scarlet twice-dyed threads and interwoven with gold.

The Urim and Thummim are described in my study Bible as follows: In Exodus 28, God used various methods to guide the ancient Israelites, including the Urim and the Thummim. The high priest carried these objects in his "breastpiece of decision." And used them in seeking God's will (Exodus 28:29-30). Reliance on this unique means of revelation (Numbers 27:21; Deuteronomy 33:8) seems to have ceased after David's reign, although an attempt to revive the practice occurred during the postexilic period, in the fifth century B.C. (see Ezra 2:26, Nehemiah 7:65).

THE BREASTPLATE OF RIGHTEOUSNESS

The Urim and Thummim may have been small metal objects or stones or sticks inscribed with symbols, possibly the 22 letters of the Hebrew alphabet based on the fact that the first letter of Urim (aleph) and the first letter of Thummim (tau) are the first and final letters of this alphabet, respectively.

Most likely, as Biblical passages imply, the Urim and Thummim were cast as lots in order to obtain yes or no answers from God. Casting of lots is widely attested to in the Bible (Leviticus 16:8; Numbers 33:54; Proverbs 16:33; Acts 1:26). But two passages suggest that asking God a series of questions and using a process of elimination to determine His answers yielded more subtle revelation, such as a person's hiding place or a complex battle strategy (see I Samuel 10:20-22; II Samuel 5:22-24). Some Biblical historians believe that the high priest would disclose an oracle and the Urim and the Thummim would be used to confirm its truth.

Casting lots is described in my study Bible as follows: In Job 6, a clay cube inscribed in Akkadian provides archeological evidence for the use of lots in the ancient Near East. This "lot," a cube approximately one inch (2.5 cm) in diameter, commemorates the selection by lot of Iahali to serve as the minister of the Assyrian king Shalmaneser III (828 B.C.). Though other forms of divination were prohibited in Israel (Deuteronomy 18:9-14), the casting of lots was permitted. Proverbs 16:33 makes this clear: "The lot is cast into the lap, but its every decision is from the Lord." Lots were cast for various purposes.

- They settled the appointment of land, guaranteeing that it was divinely inherited (Numbers 26:55).

- They narrowed the field of candidates in determining a selection (Saul in I Samuel 10:20; Matthias in Acts 1:26), ordering of service (temple personnel in I Chronicles 24:5; Zechariah in Luke 1:8) or guilt (a clan in Joshua 7:14; Jonathan in I Samuel 14:41).

- They were used for dividing or distributing people (orphans in Job 6:27; prisoners of war in Joel 3:3 and Nahum 3:10).

- They were used to determine the will of the Lord in a particular matter (Numbers 27:21).

Remember that the Old Testament is very law bound. Priests had to continually sacrifice animals to make atonement for the sins of the people. In the New Testament, Christ is the sacrifice. After Christ's sacrifice, many of the mandatory duties (sacrificing especially) ceased. It is important to realize, however, that the breastpiece is described in detail in the Old Testament, and it must be created in a certain way with particular stones and patterns.

I say this only to highlight that making a decision was not a flippant event. Old Testament folks spent a lot of time on issues. They took them seriously and they sought the Lord! If we spent as much time simply seeking the Lord as they did creating breastplates and using the Urim and Thummim, we would be amazed at the amount of information God would reveal to us. Psalm 145:18 states, *"The Lord is close to all who call upon him– all who call upon him sincerely."*

It was also crucial that the priest did not make a decision based on his own emotions. He was trained to be able to distinguish between his own anger, fear, favoritism, desire (you name it), and the will of God. That's what we must get out of this lesson. Today, the official fancy breastplate is not part of our everyday lives. Our pastors don't show up for the Sunday sermon wearing an elaborate breastplate with expensive jewels and a fancy undershirt with gold interwoven in it. Sure, our pastors could do that for effect one Sunday to teach a lesson on the breastplate, and that would be fun, but it's not a must as it was in ancient days. Also, as Warrior Moms, we don't have to be all cleaned up and jeweled up to go to God to pray and ask Him to help us make a decision. I believe the lesson, however, is that we must take the time to seek His will.

If you want to be a trained Warrior Mom, you must take the time to distinguish between your emotions, the emotions of the world, the emotions of a friend, a family member, an enemy — just call it emotion — and the will of God. You must train yourself in the skill of differentiating between your emotions and God's will. How do you do that?

Philippians 2:12-13 states, *"Therefore, my dear friends, as you have always obeyed–not only in my presence, but now much more in my absence–continue to work out your salvation with fear and trembling, for it is God who works in you to will and act according to his good purpose."* Now, this does not mean that you are working for your salvation. No! Once saved, you are saved. The rest of your life is about seeking God's will, His guidance, and His help in all the matters you deal with. It is about being a light to the world so that others may be saved. Once saved, you are a tool of God. We don't improve our efficiency by sitting on our couches waiting to die and go to glory. We become more and more useful to His kingdom because we get up and work it out. We wake and seek Him daily! If you decide to begin a workout routine, do you stay on your couch? No, you get some tennis shoes and some comfortable clothes and you go break a sweat! This is also the case with the spiritually saved.

Now that you understand the context, what is emotion anyway? For the worldly definition, let's employ Webster again.

Emotion: intense feeling of (as in love, hate or despair).

People kill others because of intense emotion. People commit suicide because of emotion. People smoke, drink, lie, cheat, run, write, draw, create, sing, laugh, hope, cry, dance, get married, have children, pursue dreams, and do many other things because of emotion. There doesn't seem to be a distinct difference between whether someone does something extremely horrible or extremely beautiful because of emotion. Emotion to me then seems to be full of risk. You might do evil and you might do good based upon your emotions. Therefore, God must be consulted to differentiate between your emotion and His will.

About 10 years ago, when I was told that my son, Jacob, was profoundly deaf, I grappled with emotion. I was distraught, weak, defeated, and hopeless. I went on a walk and talked with God. I said, "Okay, God, I understand that I must do a lot of things for my son regarding this deaf situation, but what I'm really struggling with, what is really in the way right now is my emotion! What do I do with this emotion?! It's killing me. It feels like my foot is in my throat. It hurts so bad! I have to get rid of this emotion so I can do what I need to do for my son. So, what I am asking right now is not, 'Why is my son deaf?' but 'What is emotion!?'" God gave me an immediate answer:

THE BREASTPLATE OF RIGHTEOUSNESS

    E empty

      M moments

        O of

          T tears

            I instead

              O of

                N nonstop

                  S strength

Then, God said, "Go ahead and cry, Kristina. I made you that way. Without emotion, you wouldn't write, hope, care, create, love, or have compassion for others. Go ahead and cry. I know it hurts. But remember, after the tears, after the emotion, just remember that I am your nonstop strength. I AM."

I immediately understood that I must have emotion because I am human, but I must also remember that God is a God who is stronger than any emotion that seeks to destroy me. Since emotion is something that causes people to die or live at a 50-50 reliability rate, I want to run to God and seek His will and live at a 100 percent reliability rate! "The thief comes only to steal and kill and destroy; I have come that they may have life, and have it to the full." (John 10:10)

"Forgetting what is behind and straining toward what is ahead, I press on toward the goal to win the prize for which God has called me heavenward in Christ Jesus. All of us who are mature should take view of such things. And if on some point you think differently, that too God will make clear to you. Only let us live up to what we have already attained. Join with others in following my example, brothers, and take note of those who live according to the pattern we gave you. For, as I have often told you before and now say again even with tears, many live as enemies of the cross of Christ. Their destiny is destruction, their god is their stomach, and their glory is in their shame. Their mind is on earthly things. But our citizenship is in heaven. And we eagerly await a Savior from there, the Lord Jesus Christ, who by the power that enables him to bring everything under his control, will transform our lowly bodies so that they will be like his glorious body. Therefore, my brothers, you whom I love and long for, my joy and crown, that is how you should stand firm in the Lord, dear friends!" (Philippians 3:13-21; 4:1)

Their stomachs are their emotions. Whatever they feel, they act upon. But those who seek the Lord will learn to differentiate between their own earthly hunger and God's will. And you may notice as you train yourself in this that God will continually ask you to do things that are out of your comfort zone. You might be hungry for something and He'll say, "Don't eat that." You might be full of something and He'll say, "Eat more." Now, we know that I'm not talking about food here.

A Deeper, Very Important Lesson about Righteousness

1 John 2:1-2 *My dear children, I write this to you so that you will not sin. But if anybody does sin, we have one who speaks to the Father in our defense - Jesus Christ, the Righteous One. He is the atoning sacrifice for our sins and not only for ours but also for the sins of the whole world.*

Jeremiah 23:6 *This is the name by which he will be called: The Lord our Righteousness.*

Hebrews 1:8 *Your throne, O God, will last forever and ever, and righteousness will be the scepter of your kingdom.*

Christ is righteous, and He has been given all authority.

Matthew 28:16-10 *Then the eleven disciples went to Galilee, to the mountain where Jesus had told them to go. When they saw him, they worshipped him; but some doubted. Then Jesus came to them and said, "All authority in heaven and on earth has been given to me. Therefore go and make disciples of all nations, baptizing them in the name of the Father and of the Son and of the Holy Spirit, and teaching them to obey everything I have commanded you. And surely I am with you always, to the very end of the age.*

Lets check Webster's definition.

Righteous: acting or being in accordance with what is just or moral. Moral means conforming to a standard of right behavior.

Jesus is perfect. When Jesus walked on this earth, He never sinned. It makes sense that He is the Righteous One.

Hebrews 4:14-16 *Therefore, since we have a great high priest who has gone through the heavens, Jesus the Son of God, let us hold firmly to the faith we profess. For we do not have a high priest who is unable to sympathize with our weaknesses, but we have one who has been tempted in every way, just as we are – yet was without sin. Let us then approach the throne of grace with confidence, so that we may receive mercy and find grace to help us in our time of need.*

I invite you to pause here for a moment. Look up more scriptures on righteous and righteousness. You will find that Jesus is The Righteous One. It makes sense that the Breastplate of Righteousness is such a powerful piece of the Armor; it represents the righteousness of Christ. The righteousness of Christ is all-powerful, and it is because of His power working within us that we are able to stand firm against the pressures of this world, and against the pressures of emotions of the flesh. It is because He died on the cross for our sins that we are even able to approach the throne of God and ask for help.

Scriptures about Righteousness

FIELD EXERCISES

Think about this lesson as you study the following scriptures.

Isaiah 59:17 (in reference to God) *He put on righteousness as his breastplate, and the helmet of salvation on his head.*

Ephesians 6:14 *Stand firm then, with the belt of truth buckled around your waist, with the breastplate of righteousness in place, and with your feet fitted with the readiness that comes from the gospel of peace.*

I Thessalonians 5:4-11 *But you brothers, are not in darkness so that this day should surprise you like a thief. You are all sons of the light and sons of the day. We do not belong to the night or to the darkness. So then, let us not be like others, who are asleep, but* let us be alert and self-controlled, putting on faith and love as a breastplate, *and the hope of salvation as a helmet. For God did not appoint us to suffer wrath but to receive salvation through our Lord Jesus Christ. He died for us so that, whether we are awake or asleep, we may live together with him. Therefore encourage one another and build each other up, just as in fact you are doing.*

1. How will using the breastplate of righteousness help you?

   _____
   _____

2. Do you feel differently about emotions? Please explain.

   _____
   _____
   _____

3. What is the main thing that you have learned from this chapter?

   _____
   _____
   _____

4. Is there a particular scripture(s) that resonates with you? Write it down. Work to memorize the scripture.

   _____
   _____
   _____

Warrior Moms Unite! ™

CHAPTER 5

THE FRUITS OF JOY AND PATIENCE

www.WarriorMoms.net

CHAPTER 5

Now that we understand the use of the breastplate, we must also remember that the fruit of the Spirit is what nourishes a Warrior Mom in battle. We already discussed how love is the ultimate answer to any of our questions. That's why God sent His son and love is why He asks us to do things outside of our comfort zone. Love is the answer. Now that we have the answer, let's go on from here and ask How? and What? We must employ more fruits of the Spirit to do so.

While running up Collins Hill Road one day, God gave me a definition. "Joy is the invisible material with which the nails of endurance are made."

Say that a few times.

When God spoke that definition to me, I knew exactly to which verse He was referring:

Hebrews 12:1-4 *Therefore, since we are surrounded by such a great cloud of witnesses, let us throw off everything that hinders us and the sin that so easily entangles us, and let us run with perseverance the race marked out for us. Let us fix our eyes on Jesus, the author and perfecter of our faith, who for the joy set before him endured the cross, scoring its shame, and sat down at the right hand of the throne of God. Consider him who endured such opposition from sinful men so that you will not grow weary and lose heart. In your struggle against sin, you have not resisted to the point of shedding blood. And you have forgotten the word of encouragement that addresses you as sons.*

Did you notice that I happened to be running up Collins Hill Road asking God to speak to me on this matter when He gave me that definition? Did you notice that Hebrews talks about running? Do you see how what we do and who we are is not merely physical? There's so much more! God wants us to get deeper meaning and lessons out of seemingly ordinary circumstances, like running up Collins Hill. He's such a wonderful teacher because He constantly gives examples and hands-on learning experiences in the middle of our seemingly ordinary everyday lives.

Back to the fruits: Joy is the invisible material with which the nails of endurance are made. So often, people confuse happiness with joy. Happiness is based on what happens to you. If Jesus based His happiness on His circumstances, He would have been devastated, depressed, and hopeless because it didn't look so good; He was dying, nailed to a cross. And such is the case with us. During our trials, if we base our happiness on our circumstances, we will be defeated and hopeless because things don't look so good—with mere physical eyes. However, joy is the invisible material with which the nails of endurance are made! Just as Jesus knows, we also know the following:

Romans 5:1-5 *Therefore since we have been justified by faith, we have peace with God through our Lord Jesus Christ, through whom we have gained access by faith into this grace in which we now stand. And we rejoice in the hope of the glory of God. Not only so, but we also rejoice in our sufferings because we know that suffering produces perseverance, perseverance, character and character, hope. And hope does not disappoint us, because God has poured out his love into our hearts by the Holy Spirit, whom he has given us.*

THE FRUITS OF JOY AND PATIENCE

Isaiah 40:31 *Those who hope in the Lord will not be disappointed.*

So joy is not the same as happiness, and those who hope in God (not an expected outcome) will not be disappointed. Women who understand these things are the kind of warriors who can rejoice in suffering because they have a peace that surpasses all understanding!

Philippians 4:4-7 *Rejoice in the Lord always. I will say it again, Rejoice! Let your gentleness be evident to all. The Lord is near. Do not be anxious about anything, but in everything, by prayer and petition, with thanksgiving, present your requests to God. And the peace of God, which transcends all understanding, will guard your hearts and minds in Christ Jesus.*

One Sunday morning, I was up early studying peace. I had studied 20 verses or so and could not find the one I wanted. I told God, "Well, I'll trust You to reveal it to me when I get home." It didn't take until I got home; it was in Sunday's sermon! I kid you not. When Jesus rebuked the waves, he said, "Peace be still!"and the waves calmed down. The church's Bible didn't word it that way, (the church's Bible read "quiet – be still") but my Bible at home worded it with "peace – be still."

My main point is that the one verse I was searching for I got when I went to church. Out of all the verses in the Bible, out of all the things that could have been preached that day, it was the one verse I was looking for two hours earlier. A huge sense of peace came over me. I was reminded that God is in charge, and I can have peace in the midst of my storm. It's in Luke 8:24, by the way.

And when we struggle we must remember Paul.

II Corinthians 10:1-6 *By the meekness and gentleness of Christ, I appeal to you – I, Paul, who am timid when face to face with you, but "bold" when away! I beg you that when I come I may not have to be as bold as I expect to be toward some people who think we live by the standards of this world. For though we live in the world, we do not wage war as the world does. The weapons [C'mon Warrior Moms!] we fight with are not weapons of the world. On the contrary, they have divine power to demolish strongholds. We demolish arguments and every pretension that sets itself up against the knowledge of God and we take captive every thought to make it obedient to Christ.*

Let's read that again — there's huge power here:

. . . and we take captive every thought to make it obedient to Christ. And we will be ready to punish every act of disobedience, once your obedience is complete.

Our thoughts of doubt, of fear, of listening to broken records of this world, of what people have said to us, of what we have said to ourselves, and of what the enemy tries to whisper to us must be taken captive, put in chains and made obedient to Christ! Then, the sentences get turned around for the positive and for the nourishment of our souls: I can, I will, I am able in Christ! These types of sentences are those that were once negative but were then made obedient to Christ. When we have thoughts that are not nourishing, we make them captive to Christ. Then, we have the power to say, "Oh, no! No more!" Don't ever forget the power of this verse. It helps defeat depression and doubt because it allows you to be free from victim mentality, and it helps you become a victor.

LET'S RECAP

In short, God will give us the long version to our questions on the other side of glory, but for now we take the answer to our Why? as love. Love is the answer. Joy is the invisible material with which the nails of endurance are made. We then gain peace that surpasses all understanding. And patience is not possible without the first three.

 ## A VISUAL FOR YOU

Parents are more patient with their own children because they have loved them and endured pain for them from conception (labor pain is only the beginning and a foreshadowing of the pain that will play an ongoing role in parenting). This is why you don't have the same kind of patience for a stranger's child. Remember those late nights with 102 temperatures and your infant screaming inconsolably? All you felt was compassion. But a stranger's child screaming at a library or a restaurant drives you mad. This happens because it's not your child. You just don't have the same kind of patience regarding the inconvenience that a stranger's child brings.

In the spiritual realm, we must not differentiate our child, i.e., our circumstance, from someone else's trying circumstance. I am speaking here of the circumstances that God assigns to you; I'm not talking about all circumstances and all people. You are not to go around as if everyone and everything is your assignment. We will talk about this more in a later chapter (Don't Confuse All Battles as Yours.) However, if God assigned you to that situation, circumstance, or person's struggle, and you know that God did so, you are to be obedient to God, regardless of how you feel about it. He builds our endurance and patience through each act of obedience, no matter whose child or whose circumstance we get assigned to.

Hebrews 10:38 *And my righteous one will live by faith, and if they shrink back, I will not be well pleased.*

Mark 12:30-31 *"Love the Lord your God with all your heart and with all your soul and with all your mind and with all your strength." The second is this: "Love your neighbor as yourself." There is no commandment greater than these.*

LET'S RECAP

- Love is the answer.
- Joy is the invisible material with which the nails of endurance are made.
- We then gain peace that surpasses all understanding.
- And patience is not possible without the first three.
- And do you see how you must seek God's will, not your own emotion, in making decisions? Love and joy help you do this, and then peace can reside even during times that we spend outside of our comfort zones.

THE FRUITS OF JOY AND PATIENCE

 **FIELD EXERCISES**

1. How would you define joy?
   _____
   _____
   _____

2. How can joy be applied to trials?
   _____
   _____
   _____

3. How would you describe happiness?
   _____
   _____
   _____

4. In your personal journal, write about patience. Contemplate how your heart and home will be positively impacted by the fruit of patience. Use scriptures on patience to support your answer.
   _____
   _____
   _____

5. What main point(s) did you learn from this lesson and chapter?
   _____
   _____
   _____

6. Continue to think and pray about this throughout the week. Add notes and insights that you gain.
   _____
   _____
   _____

Warrior Moms helped me realize my battle is against Satan and his evil schemes. The only way to win this battle is through the armor provided by the Word of God. It encourages me to know other women are standing with me in the fight.

TRACY ARNER

WARRIOR MOM OF 2

CHAPTER 6

THE WORKOUT SHOES
FITTED FOR THE GOSPEL OF PEACE WITH THE FRUITS OF KINDNESS AND GOODNESS

www.WarriorMoms.net

CHAPTER 6

It is important that God led us through distinguishing between our emotions and His will. I realized something else: anger causes people to do things quickly, without thought. People say hateful things that they later regret. Moms can be sharp with their tongues before they realize it. Moms can blame this on exhaustion. I've done it myself, but I now know that it's more likely to happen when I forget to wear my armor or when I wear my armor without the joint-connecting component of love. People drive off in an argument, instead of staying and working it out. Some people punch walls and then realize they shouldn't have done so. Anger causes people to act thoughtlessly. In the Bible, anger is described frequently as burning. I think that's interesting because once a fire starts, it spreads quickly. Just like in the earlier tennis match, anger causes discord to double and triple in size. It is also described as something that should be controlled.

Exodus 15:7 (In the song of Moses and Miriam after they were delivered from Pharaoh's army) *In the greatness of your majesty you threw down those who opposed you. You unleashed your burning anger; it consumed them like stubble.*

Exodus 32:9-14 *"I have seen these people," the Lord said to Moses, "and they are a stiff-necked people. Now leave me alone so that my anger may burn against them and I may destroy them. Then I will make you into a great nation." But Moses sought the favor of the Lord his God. "O Lord," he said, "why should your anger burn against your people, whom you brought out of Egypt with great power and a mighty hand? Why should the Egyptians say, 'It was with evil intent that he brought them out to kill them in the mountains and to wipe them off the face of the earth'? Turn your fierce anger; relent and do not bring disaster on your people. Remember your servants Abraham, Isaac and Israel, to whom you swore by your own self: 'I will make your descendants as numerous as the stars in the sky and I will give your descendants all this land I promised them, and it will be their inheritance forever.'" Then the Lord relented and did not bring on his people the disaster he had threatened.*

Did you notice that Moses pleaded for the people? Even though God said, "Now leave me alone so that my anger may burn against them and I may destroy them. Then I will make you into a great nation." Moses still pleaded for the people.

Moses could have said, "Okay, forget them. Go ahead and make me into a great nation." He didn't though; he pleaded for the people. Moses understood that he was to "love his neighbor as himself." Warrior Moms must have this type of Moses mentality. Warriors know it's not all about them.

Exodus 32:19 (Upon receiving the tablets with the ten commandments, after leaving the above discussion with God) *When Moses approached the camp and saw the calf and the dancing, his anger burned and he threw the tablets out of his hands, breaking them into pieces at the foot of the mountain.*

Numbers 32:10-13 *The Lord's anger was aroused that day and he swore this oath; "Because they have not followed me wholeheartedly, not one of the men twenty years old or more who came out of Egypt will see the land I promised on oath to Abraham, Isaac and Jacob–no one except Caleb son of Jephunneh the Kenizzite and Joshua son of Nun, for they followed the Lord wholeheartedly." The Lord's anger burned against Israel and he made them wander in the desert forty years, until the whole generation of those who had done evil in his sight was gone.*

THE WORKOUT SHOES FITTED FOR THE GOSPEL OF PEACE WITH THE FRUITS OF KINDNESS AND GOODNESS

Judges 14:19-20 (Regarding Samson, his marriage, the betrayal of his wife with the riddle) *Then the Spirit of the Lord came upon him in power. He went down to Ashkelon, struck down thirty of their men, stripped them of their belongings and gave their clothes to those who had explained the riddle. Burning with anger, he went up to his father's house. And Samson's wife was given to the friend who had attended him at his wedding.*

II Samuel 12:5-6 (Regarding Nathan rebuking David, the rich man took the poor man's lamb and offered it as a meal to his guest) *David burned with anger against the man and said to Nathan, "As surely as the Lord lives, the man who did this deserves to die! He must pay for that lamb four times over, because he did such a thing and had no pity."*

Nehemiah 9:16-18 *But they, our forefathers, became arrogant and stiff-necked, and did not obey your commands. They refused to listen and failed to remember the miracles you performed among them. They became stiff-necked and in their rebellion appointed a leader in order to return to their slavery. But you are a forgiving God, gracious and compassionate, slow to anger and abounding in love. Therefore, you did not desert them, even when they cast for themselves an image of a calf and said, "This is your god, who brought you out of Egypt," or when they committed awful blasphemies.*

Proverbs 15:1 *A gentle answer turns away wrath, but a harsh word stirs up anger.*

Proverbs 22:24-25 *Do not make friends with a hot-tempered man, do not associate with one easily angered, or you may learn his ways and get yourself ensnared.*

Proverbs 29:11 *A fool gives full vent to his anger, but a wise man keeps himself under control.*

Proverbs 30:33 *For as churning the milk produces butter, And as twisting the nose produces blood, So stirring up anger produces strife.*

Jonah 4:1-4 (Regarding Jonah's anger at the Lord's compassion) *But Jonah was greatly displeased and became angry. He prayed to the Lord, "O Lord, is this not what I said when I was still at home? That is why I was so quick to flee to Tarshish. I knew that you are a gracious and compassionate God, slow to anger and abounding in love, a God who relents from sending calamity. Now, O Lord, take away my life, for it is far better for me to die than to live." But the Lord replied, "Have you any right to be angry?"*

Ephesians 4:26 *In your anger do not sin. Do not let the sun go down while you are still angry, and do not give the devil a foothold.*

James 1:19-25 (Regarding listening and doing) *My dear brothers, take note of this: Everyone should be quick to listen, slow to speak and slow to become angry, for man's anger does not bring about the righteous life that God desires. Therefore, get rid of all moral filth and the evil that is so prevalent and humbly accept the word planted in you, which can save you. Do not merely listen to the word, and so deceive yourselves. Do what it says. Anyone who listens to the word but does not do what it says is like a man who looks at his face in a mirror, and after looking at himself, goes away and immediately forgets what he looks like. But the man who looks intently into the perfect law that gives freedom, and continues to do this, not forgetting what he has heard, but doing it–he will be blessed in what he does.*

Matthew 5:22   *"But I tell you that anyone who is angry with his brother will be subject to judgment."*

I Corinthians 16:13-14   *Be on guard; stand firm in the faith; be men of courage; be strong. Do everything in love.*

Why all this talk of anger? We must do things in love, not anger. Anger represents the opposite of peace. When Ephesians discusses one's feet being fitted with the readiness that comes from the gospel of peace, I notice that anger is nowhere to be found. Remember how anger makes people do things quickly and without much thought? If one's feet were fitted for the readiness that comes from anger, destruction and devastation would follow. The mere fact that Ephesians talks about one's feet being fitted with peace tells us that thoughtful contemplations of peace are an essential part of the process. It means that before a Warrior Mom takes one step, she has already put into practice the essential lessons in the previous chapters of this book. She goes forward in peace, not anger. All the things you have learned thus far have equipped you to go forward in peace.

LET'S RECAP
- You've learned of God's strength, not your own.
- You've learned that His word provides life.
- You've learned to unveil lies.
- You know the truth.
- You've learned about love, joy, and patience.
- You've learned the important skill of differentiating between your emotion and God's will.
- You've learned that anger causes bigger fires to burn and causes destruction, but peace is the beautiful opposite. Respond in peace, not anger. Peace extinguishes fires of destruction.

Now that you understand anger, let's employ Webster again.

Peace: state of calm and quiet, public security under law, freedom from disturbing thoughts or emotion.

Hebrews 12:11   *No discipline seems pleasant at the time, but painful. Later on, however, it produces a harvest of righteousness and peace for those who have been trained by it.*

Ephesians 2:14-18   *For he himself is our peace, who has made the two one and has destroyed the barrier, the dividing wall of hostility, by abolishing in his flesh the law with its commandments and regulations. His purpose was to create in himself one new man out of two thus making peace, and in this one body to reconcile them both to God through the cross, by which he put to death their hostility. He came and preached peace to you who were far away and peace to those who were near. For through him we both have access to the father by one spirit.*

THE WORKOUT SHOES FITTED FOR THE GOSPEL OF PEACE WITH THE FRUITS OF KINDNESS AND GOODNESS

Psalms 119:165 — *Great peace have those who love you.*

Proverbs 12:20 — *There is deceit in the hearts of those who plot evil, but joy in those who promote peace.*

Proverbs 14:30 — *A heart at peace gives life to the body, but envy rots the bones.*

Proverbs 16:7 — *When a man's ways are pleasing to the Lord, He makes even his enemies live at peace with him.*

Proverbs 17:1 — *Better a dry crust with peace and quiet than a house full of feasting with strife.*

Isaiah 9:6 — *For to us a child is born, to us a son is given and the government will be on his shoulders. And he will be called Wonderful Counselor, Mighty God, Everlasting Father, Prince of Peace.*

Isaiah 26:3 — *You will keep in perfect peace him whose mind is steadfast, because he trusts in you.*

Ezekiel 34:25-28 — *I will make a covenant of peace with them and rid the land of wild beasts so that they may live in the desert and sleep in the forests in safety. I will bless them and the places surrounding my hill. I will send down showers in season; there will be showers of blessing. The trees of the field will yield their fruit and the ground will yield its crops; the people will be secure in their land. They will know that I am the Lord, when I break the bars of their yoke and rescue them from the hands of those who enslaved them. They will no longer be plundered by the nations, nor will wild animals devour them. They will live in safety, and no one will make them afraid.*

Micah 5:5 — *And he will be their peace.*

Zechariah 8:18-19 — *Again the world of the Lord Almighty came to me. This is what the Lord Almighty says: "The fasts of the fourth, fifth, seventh and tenth months will become joyful and glad occasions and happy festivals for Judah. Therefore love truth and peace."*

Malachi 2:5-6 — *My covenant was with him, a covenant of life and peace, and I gave them to him; this called for reverence and he revered me and stood in awe of my name. True instruction was in his mouth and nothing false was found on his lips. He walked with me in peace and uprightness and turned many from sin.*

Luke 1:76-79 — *And you, my child, will be called a prophet of the Most High; for you will go on before the Lord to prepare the way for him, to give his people the knowledge of salvation through the forgiveness of their sins, because of the tender mercy of our God, by which the rising sun will come to us from heaven to shine on those living in darkness and in the shadow of death, to guide our feet into the path of peace.*

Romans 8:6 — *The mind of a sinful man is death but the mind controlled by the Spirit is life and peace.*

I Corinthians 14:33 — *Not a God of disorder but of peace*

Galatians 5:22-26 — *But the fruit of the Spirit is love, joy, peace, patience, kindness, goodness, faithfulness, gentleness and self-control. Against such things there is no law. Those who belong to Christ Jesus have crucified the sinful nature with its passions and desires. Since we live by the Spirit, let us keep in step with the Spirit. Let us not become conceited, provoking and envying each other.*

Ephesians 2:14   *He himself is our peace.*

Philippians 4:7   *The peace of God transcends all understanding.*

Hebrews 12:11   *No discipline seems pleasant at the time, but painful. Later on, however, it produces a harvest of righteousness and peace for those who have been trained by it.*

Philippians 4:5-9   *Let your gentleness be evident to all. The Lord is near. Do not be anxious about anything but in everything by prayer and petition, with thanksgiving, present your requests to God. And the peace of God, which transcends all understanding, will guard your hearts and minds in Christ Jesus. Finally brothers, whatever is true, whatever is noble, whatever is right, whatever is pure, whatever is lovely, whatever is admirable, if anything is excellent or praiseworthy think about such things. Whatever you have learned or received or heard from me or seen in me – put into practice and the God of peace will be with you.*

Romans 5:1-5   *Therefore since we have been justified through faith, we have peace with God through our Lord Jesus Christ, through whom we have gained access by faith into this grace in which we stand. And we rejoice in the hope of the glory of God – not only so, but we also rejoice in our sufferings because we know that suffering produces perseverance, perseverance character and character hope. And hope does not disappoint us because God has poured his love into our hearts by the holy spirit whom He has given us.*

WARRIOR MOM TIP

When it comes to anger, I believe we should:

1) Stop

2) Drop and

3) Roll.

After all, if we want to put out the fire that anger has caused to burn in our hearts, situations, and/or homes, we should stop letting our emotions get the best of us. We should drop whatever self-righteous issues we are holding onto, and we should allow Jesus to roll away the stone that has blocked the dead parts of our hearts from receiving the light and truth of the gospel of peace. Sure, we will have to die to self to do so, but this is what a trained Warrior Mom does. She wears shoes fitted for the readiness that comes from the gospel of peace. By the way, once you are filled with peace, patience and goodness will flow out of you. You will be kind to those who you thought you disliked. You will be good to those who have not been good to you.

Your enemy or opponent in a particular situation (i.e., your husband, your child, your neighbor, your friend), will be baffled by your peace-filled kindness. And just like the player in the tennis match, they won't be able to continue to hurl insults at you. When you don't return volleys, it's interesting how short a match becomes. I think Romans 12 says it best:

THE WORKOUT SHOES FITTED FOR THE GOSPEL OF PEACE WITH THE FRUITS OF KINDNESS AND GOODNESS

Living Sacrifices

Therefore, I urge you, brothers, in view of God's mercy, to offer your bodies as living sacrifices, holy and pleasing to God – this is your spiritual act of worship. Do not conform any longer to the pattern of this world, but be transformed by the renewing of your mind. Then you will be able to test and approve what God's will is – his good, pleasing and perfect will.

For by the grace given me I say to every one of you: Do not think of yourself more highly than you ought, but rather think of yourself with sober judgment, in accordance with the measure of faith God has given you. Just as each of us has one body with many members, and these members do not all have the same function, so in Christ we who are many form one body, and each member belongs to all the others. We have different gifts, according to the grace given us. If a man's gift is prophesying, let him use it in proportion to his faith. If it is serving, let him serve; if it is teaching, let him teach; if it is encouraging, let him encourage; if it is contributing to the needs of others, let him give generously; if it is leadership, let him govern diligently; if it is showing mercy, let him do it cheerfully.

Love

Love must be sincere. Hate what is evil; cling to what is good. Be devoted to one another in brotherly love. Honor one another above yourselves. Never be lacking in zeal, but keep your spiritual fervor, serving the Lord. Be joyful in hope, patient in affliction, faithful in prayer. Share with God's people who are in need. Practice hospitality.

Bless those who persecute you; bless and do not curse. Rejoice with those who rejoice; mourn with those who mourn. Live in harmony with one another. Do not be proud, but be willing to associate with people of low position. Do not be conceited.

Do not repay anyone evil for evil. Be careful to do what is right in the eyes of everybody. If it is possible, as far as it depends on you, live at peace with everyone. Do not take revenge, my friends, but leave room for God's wrath, for it is written: "It is mine to avenge; I will repay," says the Lord. On the contrary: "If your enemy is hungry, feed him; if he is thirsty, give him something to drink. In doing this, you will heap burning coals on his head." Do not overcome by evil, but overcome evil with good.

Whoever came up with the count-to-ten theory when you are mad must have read the Bible. Warrior Moms, next time we are angry, we will Stop, Drop and Roll and then go forward in peace.

THE WARRIOR MOM HANDBOOK

 **FIELD EXERCISES**

Disclaimer: Anger can be destructive and dangerous. Sometimes, innocent people suffer from another person's inability to control his or her anger. Therefore, I want to mention an important point. If anyone is being abused in any way, please seek help and shelter. If your life is at risk, I do not advise applying this lesson, which is for non life threatening issues that we battle day to day.

1. Think of a situation that you are currently dealing with where you are tempted to respond in anger. Jot it down briefly.

   _____
   _____
   _____

2. Regarding the above situation, think about how you can apply the Stop, Drop and Roll theory to it.

   _____
   _____
   _____

3. Explain how you will Stop it. Find a scripture that will help you Stop it. Write the scripture below.

   _____
   _____

4. Explain how you will Drop it. Find a scripture that will help you Drop it. Write the scripture below.

   _____
   _____

5. Explain how you will Roll with it. Find a scripture that will help you Roll with it. Write the scripture below.

   _____
   _____

6. Contemplate and write down some ways that you can respond in peace.

   _____
   _____
   _____

THE WORKOUT SHOES FITTED FOR THE GOSPEL OF PEACE WITH THE FRUITS OF KINDNESS AND GOODNESS

7. Find three verses of scripture to bolster your ability to respond in peace. Write them down below.

    A. _____

    B. _____

    C. _____

8. What have you learned?

9. How are you different now than before you studied this chapter?

Warrior Moms Unite! ™

The Warrior Mom Handbook has blessed me tremendously. Through the study, I have obtained life skills equipping me with power and knowledge needed to battle all of life's problems. I have learned that we are never to fight alone. I am now armored and feel empowered!

MARLA HOLLAND
WARRIOR MOM OF 3

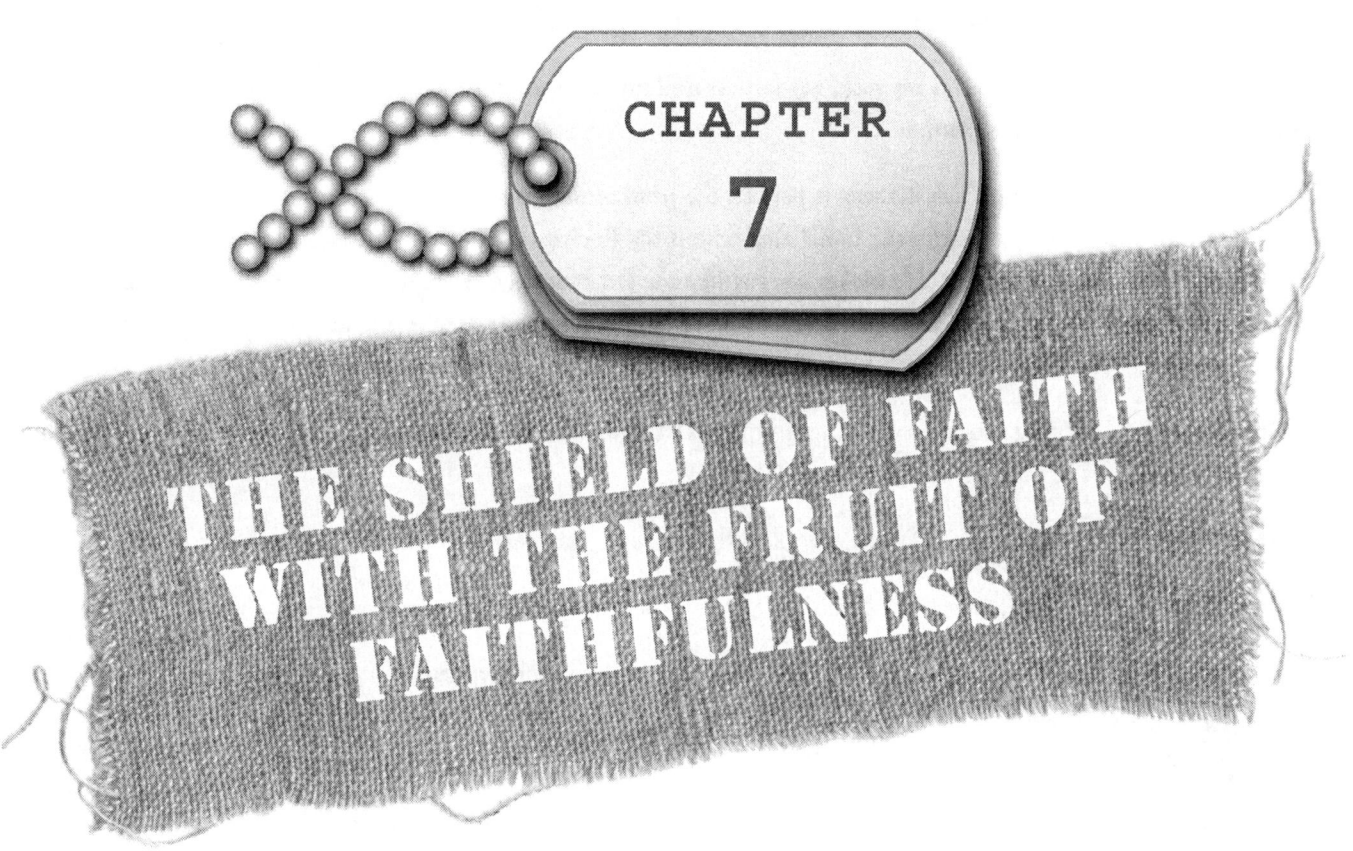

CHAPTER 7

THE SHIELD OF FAITH WITH THE FRUIT OF FAITHFULNESS

CHAPTER 7

Ephesians 6:16 *In addition to all this, take up the shield of faith, with which you can extinguish all the flaming arrows of the evil one.*

God is constantly referred to as our shield. In Genesis, He says, "*I am your shield.*" (Genesis 15:1) Time and time again, He is referred to as our shield:

II Samuel 22:2-3 *The Lord is my rock, my fortress and my deliverer; my God is my rock, in whom I take refuge, my shield and the horn of my salvation.*

II Samuel 22:31-37 *As for God, his way is perfect; the word of the Lord is flawless. He is a shield for all who take refuge in him. For who is God besides the Lord? And who is the Rock except our God? It is God who arms me with strength and makes my way perfect. He makes my feet like the feet of a deer; he enables me to stand on the heights. He trains my hands for battle; my arms can bend a bow of bronze. You give me your shield of victory; you stoop down to make me great. You broaden the path beneath me, so that my ankles do not turn.*

Psalms 3:3-4 *But you are a shield around me, O Lord; you bestow glory on me and lift up my head. To the Lord I cry aloud, and he answers me from his holy hill.*

Psalms 5:12 *For surely, O Lord, you bless the righteous; you surround them with your favor as with a shield.*

Psalms 7:10 *My shield is God Most High who saves the upright in heart.*

Psalms 18:2-3 *The Lord is my rock, my fortress and my deliverer; my God is my rock, in whom I take refuge. He is my shield and the horn of my salvation, my stronghold. I call to the Lord, who is worthy of praise, and I am saved from my enemies.*

Psalms 28:7 *The Lord is my strength and my shield; my heart trusts in him, and I am helped.*

Psalms 33:20-22 *We wait in hope for the Lord; he is our help and our shield. In him our hearts rejoice, for we trust in his holy name. May your unfailing love rest upon us, O Lord, even as we put our hope in you.*

Psalms 84:11 *For the Lord God is a sun and shield; the Lord bestows favor and honor; no good thing does he withhold from those whose walk is blameless.*

Psalms 91:4 *He will cover you with his feathers, and under his wings you will find refuge; his faithfulness will be your shield and rampart.*

Psalms 115:9 *O house of Aaron, trust in the Lord – he is their help and shield.*

Psalms 119:114 *You are my refuge and my shield; I have put my hope in your word.*

Psalms 144:1-2 *Praise be to the Lord my Rock, who trains my hands for war, my fingers for battle. He is my loving God and my fortress, my stronghold and my deliverer, my shield in whom I take refuge, who subdues peoples under me.*

Proverbs 2:7 *He holds victory in store for the upright, he is a shield to those whose walk is blameless.*

Proverbs 30:5 *Every word of God is flawless; he is a shield to those who take refuge in him.*

THE SHIELD OF FAITH WITH THE FRUIT OF FAITHFULNESS

God is a shield to those who believe in Him and have accepted His son. *"No one who denies the Son has the Father; whoever acknowledges the Son has the Father also."* (I John 2:23) Hebrews defines faith as the substance of things hoped for the evidence of things unseen. Everyone, go to the Concordance in your Bible and look up the word faith. Just read the half sentences listed there, and you'll be overwhelmed with instances and stories of faith. Over and over, Jesus is amazed at the amount of faith that some people have (Luke 7:9), and He is surprised at others' lack of faith (Mark 6:6). What is the state of your faith?

A Warrior Mom must believe in the power of her shield. That shield is God. Do you believe in the power of God? I heard someone describe faith as "stepping into the darkness and the unknown and knowing that God will provide the footing you need." If you are going to raise an invisible shield and trust an invisible God, you must believe. When I go through discouraging times I soak myself in the Word. In fact, I am writing this study from the ashes, but I know that God will lift me up from the ashes in due time. *"I waited patiently for the Lord; he turned to me and heard my cry. He lifted me out of the slime pit, out of the mud and the mire; he set my feet on a rock and gave me a firm place to stand. He put a new song in my mouth, a hymn of praise to our God. Many will see and fear and put their trust in the Lord."* (Psalms 40:1-3)

Faith is about proclaiming from the pit that God will lift you out of it! Faith is knowing that the shield you raise for protection is His righteous right hand! Faith is trusting in what you can't see. God can take nothing and turn it into something: "the substance of things hoped for" and the "evidence of things unseen." This does not say the "tangible things we trust in." It means that if you believe in the unseen, God will provide the evidence. It will manifest through God's grace as a result of faith. He wants us to trust Him in situations that we can't understand.

When my son, Jacob, was five years old, the doctors told us he would be blind by the time he was 10. I was hurled into a hands-on lesson on faith. Unable to rely on physical eyes and their abilities, I had to trust in a God who I could not see regarding my son's ability to see. No, it wasn't fun. For three months, I grappled with it all. I didn't sleep, experiencing the same nightmare over and over again.

My Nightmare

Every night, as soon as I went to sleep, I found myself in the same nightmare. I was in a jungle in Panama (I'm sure this visual came from my husband's Army pictures of when he was there with the 2nd Ranger Battalion). I was walking on an overgrown trail. The trail was covered with snakes. Some snakes were half alive, some were dead, and some were completely 100 percent alive. Every step I took revealed the percentage of life they still had in them. It was horrifying! I would make my way out of the overgrown trail only to find the Kahuna of all mother snakes (bigger than the size of a tall building in New York!) She was sleeping, but as soon as I peered my head out, she would wake up, swing her long neck around and come at me with her huge mouth wide open. I would wake up, sweating, sitting straight up in bed. Every night, it was the same nightmare. I didn't want to go to sleep, I couldn't go to sleep, but eventually I would go to sleep and find myself in the same jungle, knowing my fate. I was even aware in my dream that I was in the same dream and every time I thought, "Not again!" After three months of this nightmare, I decided I was going to get on my knees and not get up until I heard from God. I didn't care if I lost my job, and my family had to bring me food and water. I wasn't getting up until I heard from God.

You see, my main source of difficulty stemmed from the fact that I was terrified of blindness! For years, as we dealt with the deafness, I actually told people, "Well, I'm just so thankful it's not his eyes; if I had to choose between deafness and blindness, I'd choose deafness because in my mind, blindness would be the worst thing that could happen." I almost heard the haunting echo of myself saying this everyday as I looked straight ahead at the monster of blindness before my son. I told God, "I am not going to go to you like Job did and question 'Why?' I've worn out the book of Job, and I know that you spent column upon column telling Job Who set the stars and moon, stores hail, and tells the water where to stop. I don't want that lecture. I'm just going to stay on my knees until you speak, whatever you say; I must hear you speak because I cannot remain in this nightmare! I even thanked you in the deafness that it wasn't his eyes because in my mind, blindness would be the worst thing that could happen!"

I was on my knees in silence for about two hours, I think; I lost track of time. And then, out of the silence I heard, *"It is the worst thing that will NEVER happen."* His voice shocked me. I sat up and looked around. His words jolted me to attention. I sat there for a moment and repeated what He said, "It's the worst thing that will never happen... It's the worst thing that will never happen, It's the worst thing that will NEVER happen!" Then, it hit me; it won't happen! I got up off my knees and I never despaired about a diagnosis of blindness again.

But there's more. That night, I was so excited to go to sleep! I knew that I would sleep. I had peace. I had heard from God. I was almost skipping around the rest of the day! As soon as I fell asleep, however, I was back in the jungle! "What! Wait a minute! I'm not supposed to be here! God, you spoke today! What am I doing in this nightmare?!" I kept walking on the trail, knowing full well that the mama snake would see me and come at me with her mouth wide open. She did. But this time, I ran out and darted past her and around her. I thought, "Yes! This is a part of the nightmare I have never experienced. But then, there was a wall. It was a big grass and dirt wall. "Oh no, a big wall!" I muttered under my breath as I ran. I looked around for an alternate escape, but the wall was as long and tall as the air. It was endless. But then, I saw a small hole in the wall. It looked pretty small, but it was my only chance. I raced toward it, and I dove through it like I was an Olympic diver, right through it to the other side!

I woke up, sitting straight up in bed with the biggest smile on my face I have ever felt (well, except for when I received the Lord as my Savior, got married, and my children were born). I wasn't even sweating.

I never had the nightmare again. I knew that I had conquered the fear of blindness and escaped to the other side of faith. I knew that I would be able to live by faith not by sight (II Corinthians 5:7).

For nights before the breakthrough, I demanded that God come down here and wrestle with me like he did with Jacob in the Bible. "If I walk with a limp for the rest of my life, so be it! I won't let go until you bless me!" I yelled.

THE SHIELD OF FAITH WITH THE FRUIT OF FAITHFULNESS

One morning, I woke up with a kink in my hip and I actually thought it was funny. I was surprised at God's humor, but I said, "I hope this means I'm wrestling with You about this, and that You are hearing me demand that I be blessed." Have you ever been there? Have you ever been so helpless, so literally stripped of any physical security that you demand that God wrestle with you? When I first read about Jacob doing that in the Bible, I thought, "Wow, that was rude, bold, and not so smart of him." But after dealing with deafness and blindness, and after studying Jacob in the Bible, I realized that his wrestling with God was an exercise of his faith. I believe that Jacob was at a place where the physical was unable to deliver, and he needed his mighty Savior to show up and leave His powerful mark.

When Jacob was first diagnosed, the eye specialists told me that I could not donate one of my eyes to Jacob because the syndrome that he has will destroy my donated eye as well. I was left to leave it all with God. So I did (Well, I did after three months of fear and the same nightmare). Once I gave up the fight of my despair, God spoke, I stood, and now I walk by faith, not by sight. Jacob is 12-years-old at this writing. He is not blind. The specialists told us that he'd be blind at 10, and every year, they are confused, but assure us that he'll be blind soon. We make them uncomfortable because Jacob's sight makes them question their science, but I am trusting in a God that I can't see. I am trusting in a God who spoke to me, who reassured me that Jacob would always be able to see. I am trusting in a God who speaks to hearts through deafness. One does not need ears to hear God. One does not need eyes to see God. The God that I see with my eyes of faith, and the God that I hear with my heart is real. He is real! Faith is the substance of things hoped for, the evidence of things unseen!

Warriors, I cannot explain faith in any more detail. It is simple: believe! When you are in the pit, trust that God will lift you out of it. That's exercising your faith. Praise His name because He inhabits praise. Soak yourself in the Word. Matthew 17:20 states: *"I tell you the truth, if you have faith as small as a mustard seed, you can say to this mountain, 'Move from here to there' and it will move. Nothing will be impossible for you."*

The enemy will hurl insults of fear and doubt at you. He will use people, circumstances, and any means available to make you doubt. The opposite of doubt is faith. So stay on the faithful side of faith. Take negative thoughts captive as we discussed earlier (II Corinthians 10:5). Don't let them take root. Don't give them the time of day. Don't let doubt occupy space in your heart and mind. Warriors are trained to take negative thoughts captive. When you are praising God and quoting scripture, negative doubt can't stick around. If you need to, take one verse and repeat it all day long. Any time doubt creeps in, cast it out! You are a Warrior now. You can do it!

Faith without works is dead. (James 2:26) You are a warrior now and you must exercise your faith. *"For physical training is of some value, but godliness has value for all things, holding promise for both the present life and the life to come. This is a trustworthy saying that deserves full acceptance (and for this we labor and strive), that we have put our hope in the living God, who is the Savior of all men, and especially of those who believe."* (I Timothy 4:8-10)

Exercise the fact that you believe in a God you can't see with mere physical eyes, but whom you know is alive. Raise your shields of faith and extinguish doubt.

Following are some of my favorite verses regarding faith:

Galatians 3:23-25 *Before this faith came, we were held prisoners by the law, locked up until faith should be revealed. So the law was put in charge to lead us to Christ that we might be justified by faith. Now that faith has come, we are no longer under the supervision of the law.*

Philippians 1:25-26 *Convinced of this, I know that I will remain, and I will continue with all of you for your progress and joy in the faith, so that through my being with you again your joy in Christ Jesus will overflow on account of me.*

I Thessalonians 1:3 *We continually remember before our God and Father your work produced by faith, your labor prompted by love, and your endurance inspired by hope in our Lord Jesus Christ.*

II Thessalonians 1:3-4 *We ought always to thank God for you, brothers, and rightly so, because your faith is growing more and more, and the love every one of you has for each other is increasing. Therefore, among God's churches we boast about your perseverance and faith in all the persecutions and trials you are enduring.*

I Timothy 6:12-16 *Fight the good fight of faith. Take hold of the eternal life to which you were called when you made your good confession in the presence of many witnesses. In the sight of God who gives life to everything, and of Christ Jesus, who while testifying before Pontius Pilate made the good confession, I charge you to keep this command without spot or blame until the appearing of our Lord Jesus Christ, which God will bring about in his own time – God, the blessed and only Ruler, the King of kings and Lord of lords, who alone is immortal and who lives in unapproachable light, whom no one has seen or can see. To him be honor and might forever. Amen.*

II Timothy 4:7 *I have fought the good fight, I have finished the race, I have kept the faith.*

Titus 2:2 *Teach the older men to be temperate, worthy of respect, self-controlled, and sound in faith, in love and endurance.*

Philemon 1:6 *I pray that you will be active in sharing your faith, so that you will have a full understanding of every good thing we have in Christ.*

Hebrews 10:38 *"But my righteous one will live by faith. And if he shrinks back, I will not be pleased with him."*

Hebrews 11:6 *And without faith it is impossible to please God, because anyone who comes to him must believe that he exists and that he rewards those who earnestly seek him.*

James 1:2-8 *Consider it pure joy, my brothers, whenever you face trials of many kinds, because you know that the testing of your faith develops perseverance. Perseverance must finish its work so that you may be mature and complete, not lacking anything. If any of you lacks wisdom, he should ask God, who gives generously to all without finding fault, and it will be given to him. But when he asks, he must believe and not doubt, because he who doubts is like a wave of the sea, blown and tossed by the wind. That man should not think he will receive anything from the Lord; he is a doubleminded man, unstable in all he does.*

THE SHIELD OF FAITH WITH THE FRUIT OF FAITHFULNESS

James 2:14-26 What good is it, my brothers, if a man claims to have faith but has not deeds? Can such faith save him? Suppose a brother or sister is without clothes and daily food. If one of you says to him, "Go, I wish you well; keep warm and well fed," but does nothing about his physical needs, what good is it? In the same way, faith by itself, if it is not accompanied by action, is dead. But someone will say, "You have faith; I have deeds." Show me your faith without deeds, and I will show you my faith by what I do. You believe that there is one God. Good! Even the demons believe that – and shudder. You foolish man, do you want evidence that faith without deeds is useless? Was not our ancestor Abraham considered righteous for what he did when he offered his son Isaac on the alter? You see that his faith and his action were working together, and his faith was made complete by what he did. And the scripture was fulfilled that says, "Abraham believed God, and it was credited to him as righteousness," and he was called God's friend.

You see that a person is justified by what he does and not by faith alone. In the same way, was not even Rahab the prostitute considered righteous for what she did when she gave lodging to the spies and sent them off in a different direction? As the body without the spirit is dead, so faith without deeds is dead.

I Peter 5:8-9 Be self-controlled and alert. Your enemy the devil prowls around like a roaring lion looking for someone to devour. Resist him, standing firm in the faith, because you know that your brothers throughout the world are undergoing the same kind of sufferings.

Psalms 31:23 Love the Lord, all his saints! The Lord preserves the faithful.

Psalms 37:28 For the Lord loves the just and will not forsake his faithful ones.

Psalms 89:24 My faithful love will be with him, and through my name his horn will be exalted.

Psalms 97:10 Let those who love the Lord hate evil, for he guards the lives of his faithful ones and delivers them from the hand of the wicked.

Psalms 145:13-14 The Lord is faithful to all his promises and loving toward all he has made. The Lord upholds all those who fall and lifts up all who are bowed down.

Proverbs 28:20 The faithful man will be richly blessed, but one eager to get rich will not go unpunished.

Matthew 25:21 His master replied, "Well done, good and faithful servant! You have been faithful with a few things; I will put you in charge of many things. Come and share your master's happiness."

Romans 3:3-4 What if some did not have faith? Will their lack of faith nullify God's faithfulness? Not at all!

Romans 12:12-13 Be joyful in hope, patient in affliction, faithful in prayer. Share with God's people who are in need. Practice hospitality.

I Corinthians 10:12-13   So, if you think you are standing firm, be careful that you don't fall! No temptation has seized you except what is common to man. And God is faithful; he will not let you be tempted beyond what you can bear. But when you are tempted, he will also provide a way out so that you can stand up under it.

II Corinthians 1:18-22   But surely as God is faithful, our message to you is not "Yes" and "No." For the Son of God, Jesus Christ, who was preached among you by me and Silas and Timothy was not "Yes" and 'No," but in him it has always been "Yes." For no matter how many promises God has made, they are "Yes" in Christ. And so through him the "Amen" is spoken by us to the glory of God. Now it is God who makes both us and you stand firm in Christ. He anointed us, set his seal of ownership on us, and put his Spirit in our hearts as a deposit, guaranteeing what is to come.

II Thessalonians 3:3   But the Lord is faithful, and he will strengthen you and protect you from the evil one.

Hebrews 3:6   But Christ is faithful as a son over God's house. And we are his house, if we hold on to our courage and the hope of which we boast.

Hebrews 10:23   Let us hold unswervingly to the hope we profess, for he who promised is faithful.

Galatians 5:22-26   But the fruit of the Spirit is love, joy, peace, patience, kindness, goodness, faithfulness, gentleness and self-control. Against such things there is no law. Those who belong to Christ Jesus have crucified the sinful nature with its passions and desires. Since we live by the Spirit, let us keep in step with the Spirit. Let us not become conceited, provoking and envying each other.

THE SHIELD OF FAITH WITH THE FRUIT OF FAITHFULNESS

 **FIELD EXERCISES**

1. Take the time to look up three of your own verses on faith. Write them down.

   _____
   _____
   _____
   _____
   _____
   _____
   _____
   _____

2. Additional space for your own favorite verses of faith:

   _____
   _____
   _____
   _____
   _____
   _____
   _____
   _____

3. Memorize the definition of faith: "the substance of things hoped for, the evidence of things unseen" (Hebrews 11).

4. As a bonus, memorize your favorite verses of faith as well. When you work to memorize scripture, it will come back to you when you need it the most.

The following is a poem personifying faith as a flower. It came to me after studying the scriptures. I pray it blesses you.

Warrior Moms Unite! ™

Faith is a flower

That grew in a storm

Her petals faded

Her leaves became worn

But oh how she looked to the heavens

And claimed, My God will rescue me,

Great is His fame!

Yes, He is famous for His deliverance

He's famous for His grace

And assurance.

No, I can't see Him

But I know He is there

And I claim safety in Him today

I know He does care!

I'm a flower named, Faith

Can you hear me call?

I'm one of many that you can't see

In the fall.

But, oh, yes, I exist;

I'm in the ground

God is preparing me for next season

And another round.

It may seem that I exist in seasons

But really I'm always around

Sometimes I manifest in color form

Sometimes I am growing underground.

That's the reason you wonder

If I'm still here.

But, oh, my dear, I assure you

I am always here.

My name is Faith

I'm a flower that exists

As beautiful as my Father's love

For I am a creation of His.

That's why I continually reach

To touch the Son above.

Love,

Faith

THE SHIELD OF FAITH WITH THE FRUIT OF FAITHFULNESS

 **MORE FIELD EXERCISES**

1. Write a paragraph describing who you are, what you do, things you like, what you look like, your character, your personality. Describe yourself.

   _____
   _____
   _____
   _____
   _____
   _____
   _____
   _____

2. Write a paragraph describing God. (Same as above, but this time, write about God.)

   _____
   _____
   _____
   _____
   _____
   _____
   _____
   _____

3. If Faith was personified into a real live person with whom you could meet and have coffee or tea, what would she look like? How would she act? Write a descriptive paragraph about your new friend, Faith.

   _____
   _____
   _____
   _____
   _____
   _____
   _____
   _____

The Warrior Mom Handbook has changed my life. I now wake up daily and dress in my spiritual Armor of God so that I am protected from the worldly battles I face daily. I know that by having God in the battle with me, and fighting back with the Fruits of the Spirit, I can survive the war.

DAWN GILL
WARRIOR MOM OF PRE-TEEN TWINS

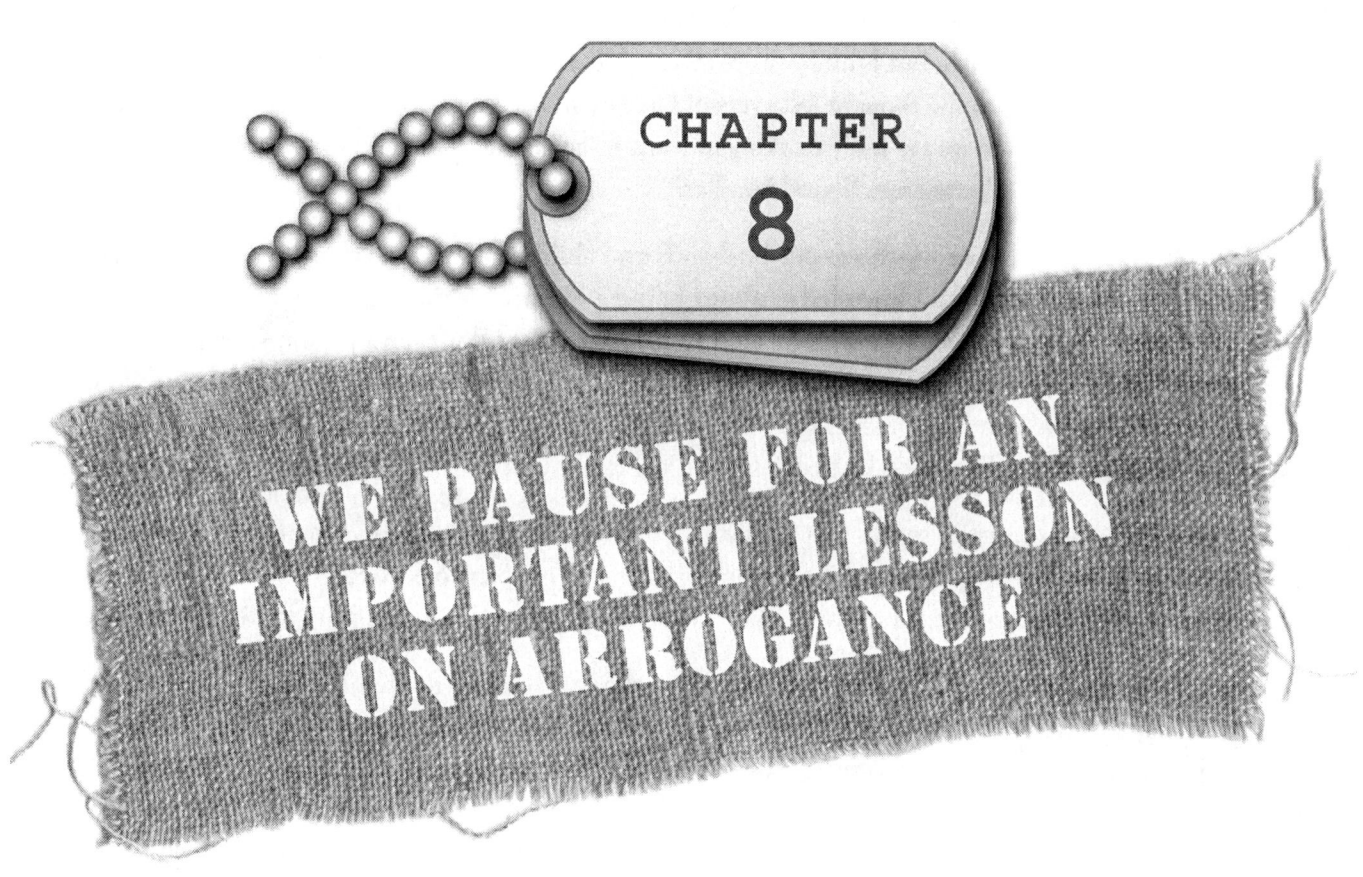

www.WarriorMoms.net

THE WARRIOR MOM HANDBOOK

When the original Warrior Moms and I first met, we were doing a study on Daniel at our church. We would listen to the sermon on Sunday and then meet to discuss the lesson in more depth. Our pastor was teaching us about having peace in a foreign land. We studied peace. He also talked of arrogance. In our arrogance, we didn't think that applied to us. You may laugh, but I think we are all capable of this. However, one of the ladies (Evie) brought up a good point. She said that she thought followers of Christ can become arrogant within their spiritual blind spots. We discussed that when we are really working to learn more about Christ and to be more like Christ, we can get irritated with those who are not. Sound familiar?

Often, the ones who receive our wrath are our husbands and children. This is a critical point! The enemy would love to use your newfound knowledge about being a Warrior Mom and defeat you with it by creating dissension in your home. You must be alert to this type of thinking, and you must be patient with those around you. They are not you, and their walk with God is their walk with God. God does not force us to be where He wants us to be. He offers the opportunities to grow, and we decide if we will receive those opportunities or not. We are to be examples of Christ, not Caesar.

Reflect upon all the lessons prior to this one. Review them if you need to, and then come back to this one. It is essential that you thoroughly understand the lessons prior to this chapter to become fully alert to how spiritual righteousness can be a tool of the enemy to defeat you and everything within this Warrior Mom Handbook.

Remember how my daughter, Faith, corrected that girl at the lunch table? Remember how I pointed out all my husband's faults? We did not emulate Christ in our actions. When God teaches us things, He does it in a loving, non-condemning way, and so should we. Remember how repaying evil with good is like putting burning coals atop one's head?

"Some of you have become arrogant, as if I were not coming to you. But I will come to you very soon, if the Lord is willing, and then I will find out not only how these arrogant people are talking, but what power they have. For the kingdom of God is not a matter of talk but of power. What do you prefer? Shall I come to you with a whip, or in love with a gentle spirit?" (I Corinthians 4:18-21)

Let's read more about arrogance.

I Samuel 2:3 *Do not keep talking so proudly or let your mouth speak such arrogance, for the Lord is a God who knows, and by him deeds are weighed.*

_____

_____

Proverbs 8:12-17 *I, wisdom, dwell together with prudence; I possess knowledge and discretion. To fear the Lord is to hate evil; I hate pride and arrogance, evil behavior and perverse speech. Counsel and sound judgment are mine; I have understanding and power. By me kings reign and rulers make laws that are just; by me princes govern, and all nobles who rule on earth. I love those who love me, and those who seek me find me.*

_____

_____

WE PAUSE FOR AN IMPORTANT LESSON ON ARROGANCE

Mark 7:21-23   *"For from within, out of men's hearts, comes evil thoughts, sexual immorality, theft, murder, adultery, greed, malice, deceit, lewdness, envy, slander, arrogance and folly. All these evils come from inside and make a man unclean.".*

_____

_____

II Corinthians 12:20   *For I am afraid that when I come I may not find you as I want you to be, and you may not find me as you want me to be. I fear that there may be quarreling, jealousy, outbursts of anger, factions, slander, gossip, arrogance and disorder.*

_____

_____

Psalms 5:5   *The arrogant cannot stand in your presence; you hate all who do wrong.*

_____

_____

Psalms 119:78   *May the arrogant be put to shame for wronging me without cause; but I will meditate on your precepts..*

_____

_____

Proverbs 17:7   *Arrogant lips are unsuited to a fool–how much worse lying lips to a ruler.*

_____

_____

Proverbs 21:24   *The proud and arrogant man–"Mocker" is his name; he behaves with overweening (arrogant) pride.*

_____

_____

Romans 1:21-22   *For although they knew God, they neither glorified him as God nor gave thanks to him, but their thinking became futile and their foolish hearts were darkened. Although they claimed to be wise, they became fools and exchanged the glory of the immortal God for images made to look like mortal man and birds and animals and reptiles.*

_____

_____

Romans 11:16-24   *If the part of the dough offered as first fruits is holy, then the whole batch is holy; if the root is holy, so are the branches. If some of the branches have been broken off, and you, though a wild olive shoot, have been grafted in among the others and now share in the nourishing sap from the olive root, do not boast over those branches. If you do, consider this: You do not support the root, but the root supports you. You will say then, "Branches were broken off so that I could be grafted in." Granted. But they were broken off because of unbelief, and you stand by faith. Do not be arrogant, but be afraid. For if God did not spare the natural branches, he will not spare you either. Consider, therefore the kindness and sternness of God: sternness to those who fell, but kindness to you, provided that you continue in his kindness. Otherwise, you also will be cut off. And if they do not persist in unbelief, they will be grafted in, for God is able to graft them in again. After all, if you were cut out of an olive tree that is wild by nature, and contrary to nature were grafted into a cultivated olive tree, how much more readily will these, the natural branches, be grafted into their own olive tree!*

I Timothy 6:17-19   *Command those who are rich in this present world not to be arrogant nor to put their hope in wealth, which is so uncertain, but to put their hope in God, who richly provides us with everything for our enjoyment. Command them to do good, to be rich in good deeds, and to be generous and willing to share. In this way they will lay up treasure for themselves as a firm foundation for the coming age, so that they may take hold of the life that is truly life.*

After reading each verse, I reworded it and thought about what it said and meant to me. I then brought all the reflections together, and surprisingly enough, it sounds like a prayer to protect us from arrogance (see next page).

God is so cool!

WE PAUSE FOR AN IMPORTANT LESSON ON ARROGANCE

 ## THE ARROGANT PRAYER

We pray that we will walk humbly and trust God for all things (1 Samuel 2:3). In our humble ignorance, we pray for wisdom. Fill us with more of You and less of us, that our unclean parts would be pushed and cleaned out because we admit that they are there (Proverbs 8:12-17)! Save us from petty thoughts that distract us from You (Mark 7:22). Help us to be as we would want You to find us (II Corinthians 12:20). We know You are not pleased with an arrogant heart (Psalms 5:5). Save us from the arrogant who seek to destroy us, and protect us from those who do not seek You! This we humbly ask and simultaneously praise You for in advance (Psalms 119:78). Oh, when we become arrogant with our hearts and lips, we lie to ourselves and to those around us (Proverbs 17:7). When we notice the shallow and pride-filled people, and even when we think they are that way, we forget that, in our judgment, we just proved ourselves to be as them. Protect us from such ways; guard our hearts and minds (Proverbs 21:24). We have such a tendency to want to worship what we know rather than what we don't know for sure, what we can't understand, and what we can't see. When we do that, we attempt to put You in a box and we are relying on the mere physical when in fact, You God, You are spiritual! (Romans 1:20). Oh, how nice to be saved as we work toward becoming even a better, stronger Christ-like person. Protect us from being so busy with our Christ-likeness that we become self-righteous and blind to our own "righteous" arrogant ways. Help us to be aware of our spiritual blind spots and protect us from falling into the trap of arrogance. We become such fools and reveal ourselves unprotected (Romans 11: 16-24). Oh, that we would share our wealth, knowing it's all Yours anyway and oh, that we would not qualify what we have as not enough to matter, and that those who have more would not qualify themselves as being above the smaller people and things. For it truly is the little things that matter and no people are little, and You can do ten-fold with a little, and You can grab back the ten million from the one who does not acknowledge You. Help us all to remember that no matter who we are and how little or much we have that, "He who knows he has enough is rich and he who has You is the wealthiest of all!" (1 Timothy 6:17-19) Oh, God, we pray that You would protect us with Your mighty outstretched hand of grace, from this newly revealed arrogance.

FIELD EXERCISES

During the week, reread each verse on arrogance. After you read each one, write a sentence describing what that verse means to you in the space underneath the verse. When you are all done, combine all the sentences (as I did) in paragraph form. If you want, go the extra mile and turn it into your very own paragraph prayer about arrogance.

Arrogance Paragraph Prayer

_____
_____
_____
_____
_____
_____
_____
_____
_____
_____
_____
_____
_____
_____
_____
_____
_____
_____

Warrior Moms Unite! ™

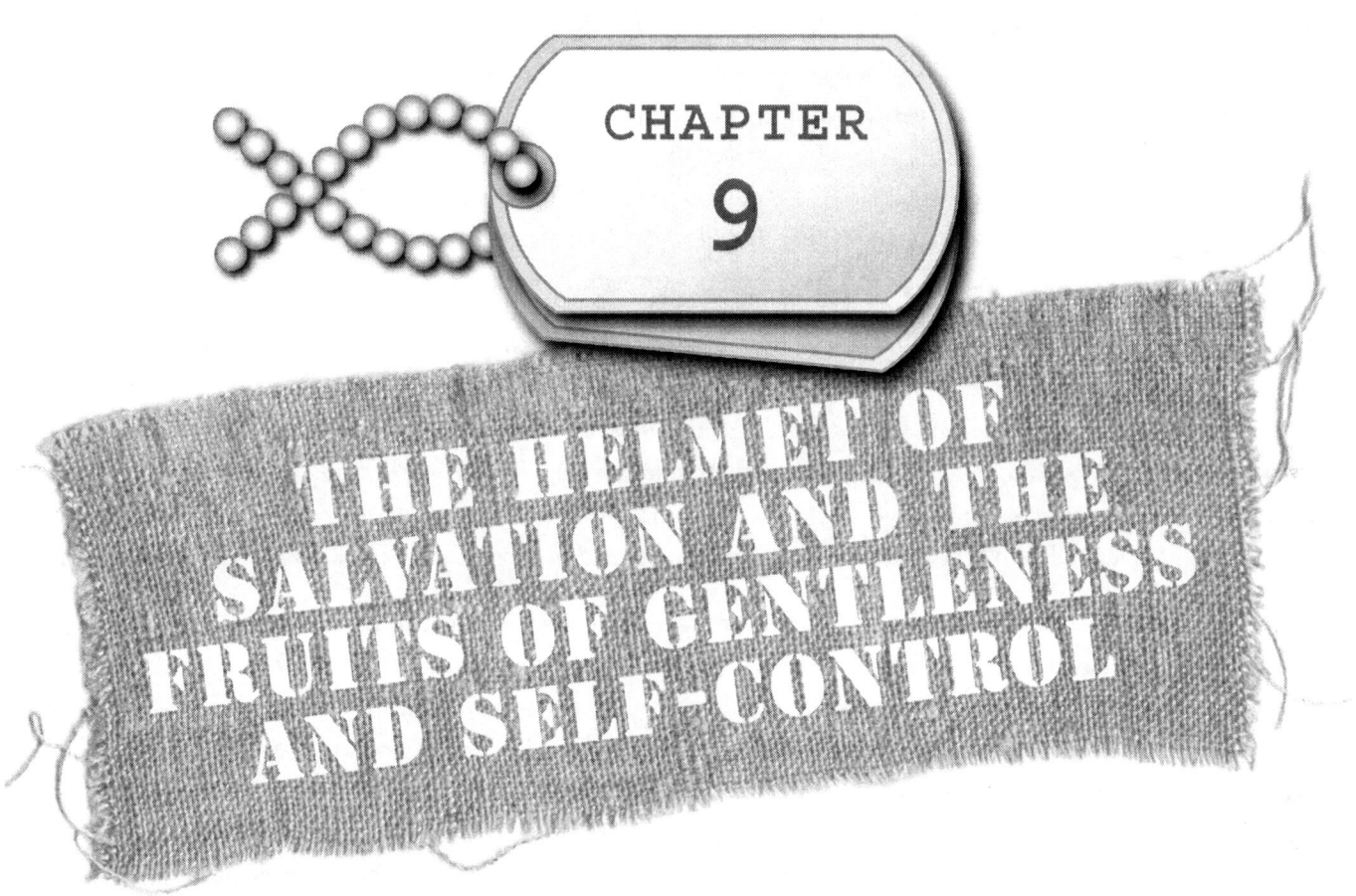

CHAPTER 9

THE HELMET OF SALVATION AND THE FRUITS OF GENTLENESS AND SELF-CONTROL

www.WarriorMoms.net

CHAPTER 9

Ephesians 6:17   *Take the helmet of salvation and the sword of the Spirit, which is the word of God.*

Isaiah 59:15-20   (In reference to the Lord) *The Lord looked and was displeased that there was no justice. He saw there was no justice. He saw that there was no one, he was appalled that there was no one to intervene; so his own arm worked salvation for him, and his righteousness sustained him. He put on righteousness as his breastplate, and the helmet of salvation on his head; he put on the garments of vengeance and wrapped himself in zeal as in a cloak. According to what they have done, so will he repay wrath to his enemies and retribution to his foes; he will repay the islands their due. From the west, men will fear the name of the Lord, and from the rising of the sun, they will revere his glory. For he will come like a pent-up flood that the breath of the Lord drives along. "The Redeemer will come to Zion, to those in Jacob who repent of their sins," declares the Lord.*

I Thessalonians 5:5-11   *You are all sons of the light and sons of the day. We do not belong to the night or to the darkness. So then, let us not be like others, who are asleep, but let us be alert and self-controlled. For those who sleep, sleep at night, and those who get drunk, get drunk at night. But since we belong to the day, let us be self-controlled, putting on faith and love as a breastplate, and the hope of salvation as a helmet. For God did not appoint us to suffer wrath but to receive salvation through our Lord Jesus Christ. He died for us so that, whether we are awake or asleep, we may live together with him. Therefore, encourage one another and build each other up, just as in fact you are doing.*

There are only three verses in my Concordance that include the word helmet. In preparing this study, I thought about wearing a helmet and asked myself, "What is protected with the helmet?" The mind, of course. So, I knew that we were to study the mind. If you think about it, don't you battle with your mind more than anything else? Don't you battle with thoughts? I know we've talked about doubt being hurled at you in various forms, but thoughts in your own mind can be a real battleground. Henry Ford said, "Every great accomplishment begins with the decision to try." We can see that if someone quits in her mind, the thought is never able to reach magnificent results — or magnificent defeat (and we learn such valuable lessons when we fail—mainly our faith grows). What I'm saying is this: If the thought gets stopped in the mind, it never gets to be a magnificent anything! So, let's study the mind.

Deuteronomy 28:65-67   (Regarding curses for disobedience) *There the Lord will give you an anxious mind, eyes weary with longing, and a despairing heart. You will live in constant suspense, filled with dread both night and day, never sure of your life. In the morning you will say, "If only it were evening!" and in the evening, "If only it were morning!" because of the terror that will fill your hearts and sights that your eyes will see."*

I Chronicles 28:9-10   *And you, my son Solomon, acknowledge the God of your father, and serve him with wholehearted devotion and with a willing mind, for the Lord searches every heart and understands every motive behind the thoughts. If you seek him, he will be found by you; but if you forsake him, he will reject you forever. Consider now, for the Lord has chosen you to build a temple as a sanctuary. Be strong and do the work.*

II Chronicles 30:12   (Regarding Hezekiah celebrating the Passover) *Also in Judah the hand of God was on the people to give them unity of mind to carry out what the king and his officials had ordered, following the word of the Lord.*

THE HELMET OF SALVATION AND THE FRUITS OF GENTLENESS AND SELF-CONTROL

Psalms 26:2-3 Test me O Lord, and try me, examine my heart and my mind; for your love is ever before me, and I walk continually in your truth.

Isaiah 26:3 You will keep in perfect peace him whose mind is steadfast, because he trusts in you.

Jeremiah 17:10 I the Lord search the heart and examine the mind, to reward a man according to his conduct, according to what his deeds deserve.

Matthew 22:37-40 Jesus replied, "Love the Lord your God with all your heart and with all your soul and with all your mind. This is the first and greatest commandment. And the second is like it: Love your neighbor as yourself. All the Law and the Prophets hang on these two commandments."

Mark 12:30-31 "Love the Lord your God with all your heart and with all your soul and with all your mind and with all your strength. The second is this: Love your neighbor as yourself. There is no commandment greater than these."

Luke 10:27 He answered: "Love the Lord your God with all your heart and with all your soul and with all your strength and with all your mind; and, Love your neighbor as yourself."

Acts 4:32-35 All the believers were one in heart and mind. No one claimed that any possession was his own, but they shared everything they had. With great power the apostles continued to testify to the resurrection of the Lord Jesus, and much grace was upon them all. There were no needy persons among them. For from time to time those who owned lands or houses sold them, brought the money from the sales and put it at the apostles' feet, and it was distributed to anyone as he had need.

Romans 7:14-25 (Regarding struggling with sin) We know that the law is spiritual; but I am unspiritual, sold as a slave to sin. I do not understand what I do. For what I want to do I do not do, but what I hate I do. And if I do what I do not want to do, I agree that the law is good. As it is, it is no longer I myself who do it, but it is sin living in me. I know that nothing good lives in me, that is, in my sinful nature. For I have the desire to do what is good, but I cannot carry it out. For what I do is not the good I want to do; no, the evil I do not want to do – this I keep on doing. Now if I do what I do not want to do, it is no longer I who do it, but it is sin living in me that does it. So I find this law at work: When I want to do good, evil is right there with me. For in my inner being I delight in God's law; but I see another law at work in the members of my body, waging war against the law of my mind and making me a prisoner of the law of sin at work within the members. What a wretched man I am! Who will rescue me from this body of death? Thanks be to God – through Jesus Christ our Lord!

Romans 8:5-8 Those who live according to the sinful nature have their minds set on what the nature desires; but those who live in accordance with the Spirit have their minds set on what the Spirit desires. The mind of a sinful man is death, but the mind controlled by the Spirit is life and peace, the sinful mind is hostile to God. It does not submit to God's law, nor can it do so. Those controlled by the sinful nature cannot please God.

Romans 12:2 *Do not conform any longer to the pattern of this world, but be transformed by the renewing of your mind. Then you will be able to test and approve what God's will is – his good, pleasing and perfect will.*

Romans 14:13 *Therefore let us stop passing judgment on one another. Instead, make up your mind not to put any stumbling block or obstacle in your brother's way.*

I Corinthians 1:10-12 *I appeal to you brothers, in the name of our Lord Jesus Christ, that all of you agree with one another so that there may be no division among you and that you may be perfectly united in mind and thought. My brothers, some from Chloe's household have informed me that there are quarrels among you. What I mean is this: One of you says, "I follow Paul"; another, "I follow Apollos"; another, "I follow Cephas"; still another, "I follow Christ."*

We must pause here for a moment. Do you see how people in the Bible struggled with their thoughts? We all struggle the same way today. If you are struggling with thoughts, it would make sense that the woman sitting next to you is struggling with thoughts as well. Now add in the fact that we all have our own junk. We all have our own hurts, insecurities, fears, blind spots about ourselves, triggers, etc. How complicated it becomes then when we all get together!

As a new Christian, I was hurt by some women in the church. I was snubbed like I was in a high school classroom rather than in a 9 a.m. Bible study. I was shocked because I was at church! Let's get real for a moment. If imperfect women are getting together to study the Word, there may be hurt feelings. Sometimes women hurt other women on purpose. A lot of times, women hurt other women and don't realize it. This happens because we have our own issues, and sometimes someone says something that strikes a nerve that is connected to an old hurt within us.

Think about your marriage or any other close relationship. Does your husband or your friend, sister, mom, etc. hurt your feelings sometimes and he or she doesn't even know it happened? Be alert! Use what you've learned in this study in all aspects of your life and in all relationships. When someone hurts you, you may need to let him or her know.

If you're participating in a Bible study and your leader hurts your feelings, she would like to know. Maybe she can learn how to do something differently next time. On the other hand, perhaps you will tell her that she hurt your feelings and she will understand that it is not she who hurt you, but someone in your past or present who hurt you. Maybe the way she said something simply reminded you of that hurt.

I am direct and I don't believe in playing games. A lot of times when wounds are fresh, the tiniest piece of salt hurts us. When I was first told that Jacob was deaf, I used to cry when I heard someone say, "What, are you deaf?" or "Oh, I must be deaf today." I'm sure there are things that you're going through right now that you are highly sensitive about.

We must be aware of these mind games, both intentional and unintentional. They are traps that the enemy sets up for the purely physically focused person. Games are simply a way for the enemy to distract you from what is really at stake here: souls. I am saying all of this now - deep within the study - because I believe that you can now digest it because of the spiritual maturity you have developed. Be alert to your own feelings, your own hurts, and how you interact.

If you are studying The Warrior Mom Handbook with a group of women, be aware that the enemy would love to cause such dissension that you will quit. He would like you to get really upset with someone so that the growth God has for you will be thwarted. If someone has already left the study due to discord or conflict within the group, call her and invite her back! Email her and ask her to read this chapter.

On a practical level:

1. If you feel hurt, pray about it.

2. Ask God to reveal to you whether this is your issue (something that you need to work on within yourself) or if this is an issue that needs to be addressed within the group.

Sometimes we need to confront people. I don't believe in pretending that big, blue elephants aren't in the room. I also don't believe in taking a mouse and making a lion out of it. This is a very important issue, and it creeps in at your blind spots. Be alert and apply this concept in your life. This can be a real issue within your marriage, your relationships, with your children, your friends, your family, and/or your co-workers. If you can get this, you will be spared from many distracting battles.

A VISUAL FOR YOU

A friend of mine was talking to me about how the ladies at the church hurt her feelings and how she just didn't want to go anymore. "I'm done with this, Kristina. I'm tired of putting myself out there and just getting hurt by women who are petty, and who frankly aren't really working on their walk with God. I don't want to keep going to church or doing the study. My husband is tired of it too. We were talking about just quitting."

I gave her a visual. I was running this summer, and I was really excited when I finally worked my way up to running two miles. My daughter, Faith, wanted to run with me one day. Faith is a natural runner. She could run a seven-minute mile flat. As we were running, it was obvious that I was holding her back. I told her to go on up ahead. When she was a good distance ahead of me, she turned around and said, "Mom, do you want me to wait?" I waved her back to me. As soon as she got back to me I said, "Faith, don't ever pace yourself based on the person behind you, even if it's your mom!"

I talked with my friend about how I know it's discouraging to get hurt by other women or anyone for that matter, but that we must not gauge our spiritual growth—or our personal growth—upon those behind us or around us. We must pace ourselves on God. God sets the pace for us, and He constantly pulls us onward.

Consider the following verses:

Philippians 3:12-14   *"Not that I have already obtained all this, or have already been made perfect, but I press on to take hold of that which Christ Jesus took hold of in me. Brothers, I do not consider myself yet to have taken hold of it. But one thing I do: Forgetting what is behind and straining toward what is ahead, I press on toward the goal to win the prize for which God has called me heavenward in Christ Jesus."*

I Corinthians 9:24-27   *Do you not know that in a race all runners run, but only one gets the prize? Run in such a way as to get the prize. Everyone who competes in the games goes into strict training. They do it to get a crown that will not last; but we do it to get a crown that will last forever. Therefore I do not run like a man running aimlessly; I do not fight like a man beating the air. No, I beat my body and make it my slave so that after I have preached to others, I myself will not be disqualified for the prize*

Hebrews 12:1-3   *Therefore, since we are surrounded by such a great cloud of witnesses, let us throw off everything that hinders and the sin that so easily entangles, and let us run with perseverance the race marked out for us. Let us fix our eyes on Jesus, the author and perfecter of our faith, who for the joy set before him endured the cross, scorning its shame, and sat down at the right hand of the throne of God. Consider him who endured such opposition from sinful men, so that you will not grow weary and lose heart.*

In summary, don't let petty thoughts of yours or someone else's entangle you. Ask the warrior within if she really wants to give in to pettiness. I'll bet she'd say, "No way!"

Let us continue to study the mind.

Colossians 2:18   *Do not let anyone who delights in false humility and the worship of angels disqualify you for the prize. Such a person goes into great detail about what he has seen, and his unspiritual mind puffs him up with idle notions.*

I Corinthians 2:6-10   *We do, however, speak a message of wisdom among the mature, but not the wisdom of this age or of the rulers of this age, who are coming to nothing. No, we speak of God's secret wisdom, a wisdom that has been hidden and that God destined for our glory before time began. None of the rulers of this age understood it, for if they had, they would not have crucified the Lord of glory. However, it is written: "No eye has seen, no ear has heard, no mind has conceived what God has prepared for those who love him." But God has revealed it to us by his Spirit.*

I Corinthians 14:14-15   *For if I pray in a tongue, my spirit prays, but my mind is unfruitful. So what shall I do? I will pray with my spirit, but I will also pray with my mind; I will sing with my spirit, but I will also sing with my mind.*

II Corinthians 13:11   *Listen to my appeal, be of one mind, live in peace. And the God of peace will be with you.*

Philippians 3:19   *Their destiny is destruction, their god is their stomach, and their glory is their shame. Their mind is on earthly things.*

THE HELMET OF SALVATION AND THE FRUITS OF GENTLENESS AND SELF-CONTROL

Hebrews 7:20-25 (Regarding Jesus, the great high priest) *And it was not without an oath! Others became priests without any oath, but he became a priest with an oath when God said to him: "The Lord has sworn and will not change his mind: 'You are a priest forever.'" Because of this oath, Jesus has become the guarantee of a better covenant. Now there have been many of those priests, since death prevented them from continuing in office; but because Jesus lives forever, he has a permanent priesthood. Therefore, he is able to save completely those who come to God through him, because he always lives to intercede for them.*

I love that last phrase because Jesus lives to intercede for us. Do you see how the battle is not our own?

I Peter 4:7-11 *The end of all things is near. Therefore be clear-minded and self-controlled so that you can pray. Above all, love each other deeply, because love covers a multitude of sins. Offer hospitality to one another without grumbling. Each one should use whatever gift he has received to serve others, faithfully administering God's grace in its various forms. If anyone speaks, he should do it as one speaking the very words of God. If anyone serves, he should do it with the strength God provides, so that in all things God may be praised through Jesus Christ. To him be the glory and the power forever and ever. Amen.*

Luke 24:37-39 (Jesus appears to his disciples after his resurrection) *They were startled and frightened, thinking they saw a ghost. He said to them, "Why are you troubled, and why do doubts rise in your minds? Look at my hands and my feet. It is I myself! Touch me and see; a ghost does not have flesh and bones, as you see I have."*

Luke 24:45-49 *Then he opened their minds so they could understand the Scriptures. He told them, "This is what is written: The Christ will suffer and rise from the dead on the third day, and repentance and forgiveness of sins will be preached in his name to all nations, beginning at Jerusalem. You are witnesses of these things. I am going to send you what my Father has promised; but stay in the city until you have been clothed with power from on high."*

Ephesians 4:17-24 *So I tell you this, and insist on it in the Lord, that you must no longer live as the Gentiles do, in the futility of their thinking. They are darkened in their understanding and separated from the life of God because of the ignorance that is in them due to the hardening of their hearts. Having lost all sensitivity, they have given themselves over to sensuality so as to indulge in every kind of impurity, with a continual lust for more. You, however, did not come to know Christ this way. Surely you heard of him and were taught in him in accordance with the truth that is in Jesus. You were taught, with regard to your former way of life, to put off your old self, which is being corrupted by its deceitful desires; to be made new in the attitude of your minds; and to put on the new self, created to be like God in true righteousness and holiness.*

Colossians 3:2 *Set your minds on things above, not on earthly things.*

Hebrews 8:10 *"This is the covenant I will make with the house of Israel after that time, declares the Lord. I will put my laws in their minds and write them on their hearts."*

I Peter 1:13-16 *Therefore, prepare your minds for action; be self-controlled; set your hope fully on the grace to be given you when Jesus Christ is revealed. As obedient children, do not conform to the evil desires you had when you lived in ignorance. But just as he who called you is holy, so be holy in all you do; for it is written; "Be holy, because I am holy."*

Revelation 2:23   *"Then all the churches will know that I am he who searches hearts and minds, and I will repay each of you according to your deeds."*

The world loves logic: If A then B. Logic helps us come up with solutions to linear equations. I believe that the mind can get in the way of the spiritual because the mind always wants a logical answer. The world teaches that if the mind has an answer, then the mind has peace. If the mind (A) has a logical answer, then the mind (B) has peace. Whereas the heart may be more easily misled by emotions, I believe that the mind may be more easily misled by its quest for logical answers. The only problem with that equation is that faith is not logical. However, we are faced with a new struggle being waged against us within our minds.

Logic is fabulous for science, but logic and love don't mix. The things we do for the sake of love do not make logical sense. Did it make logical sense that Jesus stayed on the cross when He had the power to get down from that cross? Why did He stay on the cross? As we discussed earlier: Love (i.e., God) is the answer. Love (i.e., God), not logic, held Jesus on that cross, and Love (i.e., God), not logic, holds the armor of God together. Love (i.e., God) gives soldiers the strength to endure battles and wars.

Have you ever dealt with a teenage daughter? If you don't have one, that's okay. You probably know somebody who does, and I'm sure that you were a teenage girl at some point. We could even reference the movie *Freaky Friday* to get a taste of a mother/daughter relationship. This is a good example, because emotions are all over the place for both the mom and the daughter. If a mom tries to logically explain something to her teenage daughter, the daughter's eyes roll. The mom may as well be speaking a foreign language. Then, the dad might try to jump in there and logically figure out what in the world is going on between the mom and the daughter, but he just ends up making things worse because he doesn't get the fact that while all these levels may look like a simple calculus problem, it can't be solved in black-and-white logical terms. Applying logic to try to figure out the many facets of a mother/daughter relationship is like mixing oil and water!

So, here's a linear equation for some spiritual logic:
$$Love = A$$
$$God = B$$
$$Word = A \,\&\, B$$
$$A = B$$
$$B = A$$
$$W = B$$
$$W = A$$
$$B = W$$
$$A = W$$
So: $A + B + W = C$ or $A + C + W = B$
C = A clear mind!
Write it any way you want:
$B + A = C$ and/or W $C + B = A$ and/or W $B + C = A$ and/or W $A + C = B$ and/or W

THE HELMET OF SALVATION AND THE FRUITS OF GENTLENESS AND SELF-CONTROL

You could write it a hundred ways, but the answer is always the same: Love, God, the Word — they are all the same! A math teacher will read this and say, "What?!" But a Warrior Mom could explain it to the math teacher. She might just have to say, "I know it's hard; it's spiritual calculus after all!" My point is that the world does not believe that love is a logical answer. Warrior Moms understand that, on a spiritual level, love makes perfect logical sense. *"The man without the Spirit does not accept the things that come from the Spirit of God, for they are foolish to him, and he cannot understand them, because they are spiritually discerned."* (I Corinthians 2:14)

As a Warrior Mom who understands the complicated elements of relationships, from her teenage daughter to her husband to her son to her friend to her enemy, she knows that her mind must be saturated with the things of God rather than the things of this world. The world will try to get her to believe that this is about her. This is just a trick because if a Warrior Mom makes it about herself, the focus will no longer be on God. As a result, the world's way of thinking will invade her mind. Then she will have her feelings hurt, she will feel defeated, and she will want to be heard at all costs. After all, "It's about me, right?"

All you have to do is pick up a remote and flip through a few channels to see the obsession with "It's all about me." Warrior Moms must learn to take themselves (i.e., our fleshly hyper sensitivity) out of the equation. When your teenage daughter hurts your feelings, remind yourself, "This is not about me." Granted, you may need to correct her, take her cell phone away, and talk to her about respecting authority figures, but you don't throw yourself on your bed and cry in your room for thirty minutes because she hurt your feelings.

I'm not saying that you can't get your feelings hurt. You are human. I get my feelings hurt too, especially by those whom I love deeply. But, the difference between a Warrior Mom and a regular mom is that the Warrior Mom understands that this is not about her. She understands that this is about the fact that her daughter has yet to understand the lessons in this handbook. It is really about the bigger picture! A Warrior Mom operates on a higher level. She's not arrogant about the fact that she operates on a higher level, but she understands that these issues are not occurring on a mere physical level. Warrior Moms learn how to soar above the storm.

It takes a lot of self-control to pull this off. Many young girls and women respond to situations in ways that show they lack self-control. I could share examples of the girls at my daughter's middle school who are just "spazzing and flopping around" in response to situations. Look at the women on reality shows! I won't even go there! Think about women you know who seem to react in an over-emotional way or mindless way to situations. Think of a two year old who demands a cookie before dinner. The parent says, "No, we are about to eat dinner." The two year old proceeds to throw her/himself down and roll around on the floor. *"When I was a child, I talked like a child, I thought like a child, I reasoned like a child. When I became a man, I put childish ways behind me."* (I Corinthians 13:11) The fact of the matter is that the two year old, the middle school girls, and/or those other women don't get it.

Time, maturity, and growth must occur for lessons of self-control to be mastered. When you focus on all the things that scripture says about the mind, you are more able to control yourself as you deal with the distractions, devastations, and hurts that relationships in your life will inflict upon you. I have been teaching my daughter, Faith, the concepts within this book.

She has come to understand that mean girls and/or boys who are bullies are simply people who don't love themselves, so they can't love others. She has had to rely upon Jesus as her ultimate friend. She has learned that these battles that she faces are not about flesh and blood but about souls fighting and dying around the topic of eternal life.

Fortunately, she has also come to understand that the Lord fights battles for her. The Lord lives to intercede for her. She has come to understand the meaning of her name: Faith – the substance of things hoped for, the evidence of things unseen. While she has had to deal with changes in her body, hormones, and all the fun that being a teenager brings, she has also experienced a definite maturing of her faith. She has gained an edge on other kids. Warrior Moms have an edge on this world too. When Warrior Moms understand the spiritual calculus that I discussed earlier, the complicated issues that seem like worldly calculus become simple addition problems.

The Situation + Faith (and the power of God's grace) = Victory! $S + F(G) = V$

That was a long way of describing that the helmet of salvation is a piece of armor that protects the saved from being distracted by the mind games of this world.

Self-control is a fruit that becomes evident in the life of a Warrior Mom who understands spiritual calculus.

Self-Control

Proverbs 25:28 *Like a city whose walls are broken down is a man who lacks self-control.*

Acts 24:25 *As Paul discoursed on righteousness, self-control and the judgment to come, Felix was afraid and said, "That's enough for now!"*

I Corinthians 7:5 (Regarding marriage and intimate relations with your spouse) *Do not deprive each other except by mutual consent and for a time, so that you may devote yourself to prayer. Then come together again so that Satan will not tempt you because of your lack of self-control.*

Galatians 5:22-23 *But the fruit of the Spirit is love, joy, peace, patience, kindness, goodness, faithfulness, gentleness, and self-control.*

II Timothy 3:1-5 *But mark this: There will be terrible times in the last days. People will be lovers of themselves, lovers of money, boastful, proud, abusive, disobedient to their parents, ungrateful, unholy, without love, unforgiving, slanderous, without self-control, brutal, not lovers of good, treacherous, rash, conceited, lovers of pleasure rather than lovers of God having a form of godliness but denying its power. Have nothing to do with them."*

II Peter 1:5-8 *For this very reason, make every effort to add to your faith goodness; and to goodness, knowledge; and to knowledge, self-control; and to self-control, perseverance; and to perseverance, godliness; and to godliness, brotherly kindness; and to brotherly kindness, love. For if you possess these qualities in increasing measure, they will keep you from being ineffective and unproductive in your knowledge of our Lord Jesus Christ.*

THE HELMET OF SALVATION AND THE FRUITS OF GENTLENESS AND SELF-CONTROL

Self-Controlled

I Thessalonians 5:6   So, let us not be like others who are asleep; but let us be alert and self-controlled.

I Timothy 3:2-3   (Regarding overseers and deacons) Now the overseer must be above reproach, the husband of but one wife, temperate, self-controlled, respectable, hospitable, able to teach, not given to drunkenness, not violent but gentle, not quarrelsome, not a lover of money.

Titus 1:7-9   Since an overseer is entrusted with God's work, he must be blameless—not overbearing, not quick tempered, not given to drunkenness, not violent, not pursuing dishonest gain. Rather, he must be hospitable, one who loves what is good, who is self-controlled, upright, holy and disciplined. He must hold firmly to the trustworthy message as it has been taught, so that he can encourage others by sound doctrine and refute those who oppose it.

Titus 2:1-15   (Regarding what must be taught to various groups) You must teach what is in accord with sound doctrine. Teach older men to be temperate, worthy of respect, self-controlled, and sound in faith, in love and in endurance. Likewise, teach the older women to be reverent in the way they live, not to be slanderers or addicted to much wine, but to teach what is good. Then they can train the younger women to love their husbands and children, to be self-controlled and pure, to be busy at home, to be kind, and to be subject to their husbands, so that no one will malign the word of God. Similarly, encourage the young men to be self-controlled. In everything set them an example by doing what is good. In your teaching show integrity, seriousness and soundness of speech that cannot be condemned, so that those who oppose you may be ashamed because they have nothing bad to say about us. Teach slaves to be subject to their masters in everything, to try to please them, not to talk back to them, and not to steal from them, but show that they can be fully trusted, so that in every way they will make the teaching about God our Savior attractive. For the Grace that brings salvation has appeared to all men. It teaches us to say "No" to ungodliness and worldly passions, and to live self-controlled, upright and godly lives in this present age, while we wait for the blessed hope—the glorious appearing of our great God and Savior, Jesus Christ, who gave himself for us to redeem us from wickedness and to purify for himself a people that are his very own, eager to do what is good. These then, are the things you should teach. Encourage and rebuke with all authority. Do not let anyone despise you.

I Peter 1:13-16   Therefore, prepare your minds for action; be self-controlled; set your hope fully on the grace to be given you when Jesus Christ is revealed. As obedient children, do not conform to the evil desires you had when you lived in ignorance. But just as he who called you is holy, so be holy in all you do; for it is written: "Be holy, because I am holy."

I Peter 4:7   The end of all things is near. Therefore be clear minded and self-controlled so that you can pray.

I Peter 5:8-9   Be self-controlled and alert. Your enemy the devil prowls around like a roaring lion looking for someone to devour. Resist him, standing firm in the faith, because you know that your brothers throughout the world are undergoing the same kind of sufferings.

Self-control is a beautiful fruit of the Spirit. I used to be a legal assistant. I had a boss who used to flip out over most things. At first, I allowed him to suck me into his flip-out event. My response only added to the negative energy level. Over time, I learned to not respond by simply standing there and observing him. After a while he would stop and look at me with an expression that silently said, "Well, why are you just standing there looking at me? Flip out too, get scared, get mad, get something, but don't just stand there!"

It was great because as soon as he realized I wasn't joining in and gave me that look, he realized his flip-out tactic wasn't working and stopped. Learning the art of self-control gave me control in that situation. I have continued to use it in many situations with many types of people. They will try to manipulate you with their behavior. They will create this energy that is so negative and chaotic, you will feel the pull to partake in it, but don't do it! Remain in control.

It goes along the same lines as the Tennis Match theory. I just love this particular fruit of the Spirit. I notice, however, that this fruit comes at the end of the list. I believe that's because you cannot have self-control if you don't have all the other ones in place. Jesus comes to my mind. Remember when he was sleeping on the boat with his disciples and a great storm came upon them?

Luke 8:24-25 *(Jesus calms the storm) The disciples went and woke him, saying, "Master, Master, we're going to drown!" He got up and rebuked the wind and the raging waters; the storm subsided, and all was calm. "Where is your faith?" he asked his disciples. In fear and amazement they asked one another, "Who is this? He commands even the winds and the water, and they obey him."*

When the fruit of self-control is evident in your life, the fruit of gentleness will beautifully flow from you as well. In the same way that a mom holds a new life, hugs a child after he's skinned his knee, or sweeps her child's bangs out of her eyes, so too will many of your daily responses be budding with a gentle touch. Imagine the petals of a blossoming cherry tree traveling in the gentle breeze to an unknown destination. So too will the traces of God's grace touch lives in immeasurable ways through your gentle response.

Philippians 4:5 *Let your gentleness be evident to all.*

Colossians 3:12 *Therefore as God's chosen people, holy and dearly loved, clothe yourselves with compassion, kindness, humility, gentleness and patience.*

1 Timothy 6:11 *But you, man of God, flee from all this, and pursue righteousness, godliness, faith, love, endurance and gentleness.*

1 Peter 3:15 *But in your heart set apart Christ as Lord. Always be prepared to give an answer to everyone who asks you to give the reason for the hope that you have. But do this with gentleness and respect, keeping a clear conscience, so that those who speak maliciously against your good behavior in Christ may be ashamed of their slander.*

Gentleness is a powerful fruit because it helps extinguish evil's wrath and prepares hearts to receive salvation. Just imagine how much your own children will be nourished through their very own Warrior Mom's gentle touch.

THE HELMET OF SALVATION AND THE FRUITS OF GENTLENESS AND SELF-CONTROL

A Very Important Point!

Self-control comes at the end of the list of fruits.

I Peter 4:7   *The end of all things is near. Therefore be clear minded and self-controlled so that you can pray.*

One essential thing that you need to do is pray for yourself, your family, your team, and the members of your group, but you need to specifically pray for protection from evil. Consider how Jesus prayed.

Matthew 6:9-13   *"This is then how you should pray: 'Our Father in heaven, hallowed be your name, your kingdom come, your will be done on earth as it is in heaven. Give us today our daily bread. Forgive us our debts, as we also have forgiven our debtors. And lead us not into temptation, but deliver us from the evil one.' "*

At this writing, The Warrior Mom Handbook (the first book of the Warrior series) is three years old. I now rise every morning and pray for blessings, expanded territory, and protection from evil for myself and all whom I know and love. I call aloud my prayer requests and their names to God. If you haven't read *The Prayer of Jabez* by Bruce Wilkinson, I highly suggest that you do. In fact, all of his books are strong Biblical teachings that will further equip you in your walk. I was re-reading *The Prayer of Jabez* recently and Bruce discussed how, if we are praying for expanded territory for the kingdom, that means we are walking into the enemy's territory. You will soon read the chapter, "Yes, We have an Enemy," and you will learn that we need to be praying for protection from evil. As you become more involved with the Word, and as you understand more about spiritual warfare, you will realize how essential it is that you pray for protection. We don't live in fear; we live by faith; however, as warriors we take very seriously what Jesus said, and since He told us to pray and ask for protection from evil, it is important that we do just that.

Have you noticed that when you plan to do a good work for someone, the oddest things occur that may tempt you to not follow through with that good work? It's not a coincidence that things in this world come against you as you attempt to step out in faith, in love, or in service. Even when you pray for protection from evil, it doesn't mean that evil won't still approach you in some way, but it does mean that you can rest in the fact that whatever is now facing you, you can handle with Christ on your side. And, as you pray for protection, remember, the Lord is the ultimate warrior.

Exodus 15:3   *The Lord is a Warrior.*

Wise warriors pray for protection from evil daily.

FIELD EXERCISES

1. List an instance in your life, possibly with your daughter, in which you feel this lesson will help you. (It might be about forgiveness, having patience driving her to school, self-control in dealing with hurt feelings, or how she pouts and cries over math homework.) It could also be regarding your spouse, your son, your dog, your mom, your dad, your sister, your cousin. You name it.

   _____
   _____
   _____
   _____
   _____

2. How have you been trying to solve this problem? Love? Logic? Both? Will you try a different way? Which one? Love?

   _____
   _____
   _____
   _____
   _____

3. How have you done in the area of self-control? That's a tough one for most of us. What have you learned in this chapter that will help you improve your level of self-control?

   _____
   _____
   _____
   _____
   _____

4. Will you commit to pray for protection daily? I pray for protection over my first cup of coffee every morning. Just as sure as I'm going to have a cup of coffee, I'm going to pray for protection. And if for some reason, I am not able to have a cup of coffee, I will definitely remember to pray for protection.

Warrior Moms Unite!™

CHAPTER 10

THE SWORD OF THE SPIRIT

PRAY IN THE SPIRIT ON ALL OCCASIONS

CHAPTER 10

All armor has a protective measure except the sword. The sword is the Word of God, and it is also a weapon. This is why we quote scripture. Whenever Jesus was tempted, He rebuked the enemy with scripture. He also answered the enemy with scripture. The Word is sharper than a double-edged sword. "*For the Word of God is living and active. Sharper than a double-edged sword, it penetrates even to the dividing soul and spirit, joints and marrow; it judges thoughts and attitudes of the heart.*" (Hebrews 4:12)

More on the Sword

Revelation 1:15-16   (Describing Jesus) *His feet were like bronze glowing in a furnace, and his voice was like the sound of rushing waters. In his right hand he held seven stars, and out of his mouth came a sharp double-edged sword. His face was like the sun shining in all its brilliance.*

Revelation 19:13-15   (Describing Jesus) *He is dressed in a robe dipped in blood, and his name is the Word of God. The armies in heaven were following him, riding on white horses and dressed in fine linen, white and clean. Out of his mouth comes a sharp sword with which to strike down nations.*

Warrior Moms, your weapon in all situations is the Word of God. Essentially, since the Word of God is God, then God is your weapon. And we have full access to God through his Son. This is why we pray in Jesus' name.

Romans 5:1-2   *Therefore, since we have been justified by faith, we have peace with God through our Lord Jesus Christ, through whom we have gained access by faith into his grace in which we stand.*

Ephesians 2:14-18   *For he himself is our peace, who has made the two one and has destroyed the barrier, the dividing wall of hostility, by abolishing in his flesh the law with its commandments and regulations. His purpose was to create in himself one new man out of the two, thus making peace, and in this one body to reconcile both of them to God through the cross, by which he put to death their hostility. He came and preached peace to you who were far away and peace to those who were near. For through him we both have access to the Father by one Spirit.*

The Word is alive and active! Use it as your weapon. Rebuke the enemy with it. Also, use the Word to rebuke the ones that the enemy sends to you. Rebuke sickness, pain, defeat, doubt, anger, malice, jealousy, hatred, fear, and any other thing you can think of. Rebuke it with the Word of God.

An Important Point

The Word is your weapon, but don't allow the enemy to use it against you by enlisting you in hour-long debates, trying to get you to prove yourself (your worth). You will read more about this in a later chapter, "Yes, We have an Enemy." But I will use this opportunity to plant a seed and get you thinking in this direction.

Luke 4:1-13   *Jesus, full of the Holy Spirit, returned from the Jordan and was led by the Spirit in the desert, where for forty days he was tempted by the devil. He ate nothing during those days, and at the end of them he was hungry.*

THE SWORD OF THE SPIRIT AND PRAY IN THE SPIRIT IN ALL OCCASIONS

The devil said to him, "If you are the Son of God, tell this stone to become bread." Jesus answered, "It is written; 'Man does not live on bread alone.'" The devil led him up to a high place and showed him in an instant all the kingdoms of the world. And he said to him, "I will give you all their authority and splendor, for it has been given to me, and I can give it to anyone I want. So if you worship me, it will all be yours." Jesus answered, "It is written: 'Worship the Lord your God and serve him only.'" The devil led him to Jerusalem and had him stand on the highest point of the temple. "If you are the Son of God," he said, "throw yourself down from here. For it is written: 'He will command his angels concerning you to guard you carefully; they will lift you up in their hands, so that you will not strike your foot against a stone.'" Jesus answered, "It says: 'Do not put the Lord your God to the test.'" When the devil had finished all of this tempting, he left him until an opportune time.

Do you see how the enemy worked to get Jesus to prove Himself by trying to use the Word against Him? Jesus, however, knew His Word so well, that He stood firm. I also noticed that the conversation between Jesus and the enemy did not go on for ten years. I have noticed for myself and for others, however, that sometimes we get so excited about the Word and our ability to use it, that we don't realize the enemy is using it against us to engage us in endless arguments!

One of his most powerful lies is that we are not worthy. He gets us to chase our tails defending ourselves, rather than pressing onward to attain victory in a situation. For example, I talked with a friend who said she felt like she was arguing with herself and the enemy all day about whether she was worthy or not. I've done the same thing. It's good to use the Word in your defense, but if you notice that you are chasing your tail, repeating the same old thing for five hours, you might want to just stop engaging in that argument (i.e., your defense against the enemy), and start stating how mighty God is, how loving, how kind, how magnificent, how wondrous, and on and on and on. I promise you, the enemy will quit arguing with you because he doesn't want to sit around, not being able to get a word in edgewise while you praise God all day with scripture! Plug your ears to the enemy with praises to God!

Psalms 34:1-22 *I will extol the Lord at all times; his praise will always be on my lips. My soul will boast in the Lord; let the afflicted hear and rejoice. Glorify the Lord with me; let us exalt his name together. I sought the Lord, and he answered me; he delivered me from all my fears. Those who look to him are radiant; their faces are never covered with shame. This poor man called, and the Lord heard him; he saved him out of all his troubles. The angel of the Lord encamps around those who fear him, and he delivers them. Taste and see that the Lord is good; blessed is the man who takes refuge in him. Fear the Lord, you his saints, for those who fear him lack nothing. The lions may grow weak and hungry, but those who seek the Lord lack no good thing. Come, my children, listen to me; I will teach you the fear of the Lord. Whoever of you loves life and desires to see many good days, keep your tongues from evil and your lips from speaking lies. Turn from evil and do good; seek peace and pursue it. The eyes of the Lord are on the righteous and his ears are attentive to their cry; the face of the Lord is against those who do evil, to cut off the memory of them from the earth. The righteous cry out and the Lord hears them; he delivers them from all their troubles. The Lord is close to the brokenhearted and saves those who are crushed in spirit. A righteous man may have many troubles, but the Lord delivers him from them all; he protects all his bones, not one of them will be broken. Evil will slay the wicked; the foes of the righteous will be condemned. The Lord redeems his servants; no one will be condemned who takes refuge in him.*

FIELD EXERCISES

1. Using sticky notes or index cards, write down six of your favorite scripture verses that have resonated with you thus far. (Make sure you have one on protection) Put them in various places around your home, in your car, or in your purse, briefcase, pocket, or lunch box).

2. Focus on these scriptures all week. Make sure you record them in your handbook as well.

Verse 1: _____
_____
_____

Verse 2: _____
_____
_____

Verse 3: _____
_____
_____

Verse 4: _____
_____
_____

Verse 5: _____
_____
_____

Verse 6: _____
_____
_____

THE SWORD OF THE SPIRIT AND PRAY IN THE SPIRIT IN ALL OCCASIONS

The end of all things is near. Therefore be clear-minded and self-controlled so that you can pray. (I Peter 4:7)

I love that verse! It explains a very important point: you must have an understanding of all of the lessons that came prior to this one so that you can pray! People who are freaking out, freak out first. Warrior Moms understand that they must pray because freaking out is a waste of time, and it's very counterproductive.

In the movies when someone is out of control, their friend sometimes slaps them. She may say, [slap, slap] "Snap out of it! Get a hold of yourself." Or, she may throw water on her to wake her up to the reality of the situation. I like to say, "Slap me with some faith, Kristina." I will tell friends, "Slap yourself with some faith, girl!" I understand that we're all human and that it's human nature to want to freak out. Our bodies were made for a fight or flight response. When adrenaline kicks in, we feel all fired up to do something. When we don't know what else to do, it makes sense to just freak out. But a Warrior Mom knows what to do. She does a "faith slap"– not a "freak out." There's a distinct difference.

Let's compare the two:

Freak Out	Faith-Slap
• Resort to fear	• Resort to faith
• Get swayed by the storm	• Stand firm in the storm
• Set a bad example and influence others to disbelieve	• Set a positive example of your faith in God which helps others believe
• May cause illness	• Brings healing
• Causes destruction in other areas	• Causes growth and a manifestation of the faith you exhibit
• Leads to the temptations of quitting	• Leads to an increased endurance to persevere
• The storm swallows you and those around you	• The storm subsides, peace resides, and God is glorified

You notice that Ephesians 6 tells us to pray in the Spirit on all occasions. We are to pray in the sunshine, the rain, and the monsoons. I believe that real endurance and strength come from constantly training yourself through the Word. Your prayer life is the same way. The more you pray and talk to God (they are the same in my opinion), the more you will feel His presence and the more likely you are to know when He's speaking to you.

I had a hands-on lesson of this concept when Jacob was diagnosed as being profoundly deaf. When I realized that one does not need ears to hear God, I began to pray that God would speak to Jacob and tell him all the things that I could not. I asked God to speak to Jacob's heart and teach him the things that mattered in the spiritual realm. I also asked God to teach Jacob about our physical world like colors, shapes, counting, the alphabet, a cat, a dog, you name it. I prayed that God would teach him those things. I also prayed that God would teach me how to teach Jacob, in the midst of deafness!

I began to realize that God does the same for us. Our ears might work, but we may be deaf to the things and sounds of God. But when we realize that God speaks to hearts, we understand that the Spirit communicates in and through all occasions, even deafness. So to break through worldly barriers regarding our spiritual ears, we must pray in the Spirit on all occasions. The more you do it, the better you get at it, and the more attuned your spirit becomes to the heart and voice of God.

God wants us to pray to Him on all occasions because He wants us to understand that He's in all things. The more you pray and communicate with God, the less likely you are to get your will and His will confused. I always pray that my will becomes His will in such a way that I don't know the difference. I pray that His will invades my heart, and mind, and soul. I pray that I am constantly reminded to remove myself from the equation.

Oh, sure, I'm a part of it because I am in this body on this earth for this season, but it's not about me. It's about God, and I want to know His purpose for me, in each situation that comes my way, and in each battle and war to which I get assigned.

Have you ever noticed that people sound like the people they hang out with? People in the northeast usually have a distinct northern accent. People from the south have a different kind of accent. I'm from Washington state, and people up there say, "Do you guys want a pop?" However, I've been in the south for 14 years, and now I say, "Do y'all want a Coke®?" People also act like the people with whom they associate. I read somewhere that you are the average of the five people you hang around with. Makes sense, doesn't it? So, it would make sense then that God wants us to talk with Him on all occasions. This will cause us to sound and act like Him. The more we seek Him, the more we find Him. The more we find Him, the more we love Him. The more we love Him, the more we understand Him. I think those lyrics are in a song that our worship band sings on Sunday. The more we understand Him, the more we are able to respond in:

Love • Joy • Peace • Patience • Kindness • Goodness • Faithfulness • Gentleness • Self-control

The end of all things is near. Therefore be clear-minded and self-controlled so that you can pray. (I Peter 4:7)

I pray you have been praying for protection as well.

THE SWORD OF THE SPIRIT AND PRAY IN THE SPIRIT IN ALL OCCASIONS

 ## MORE FIELD EXERCISES

Take time to really think about the concepts within Chapter 10. Answer the questions below and incorporate any scripture that comes to mind. Look in your Concordance and find scripture that supports what you wrote. Actively engage in the scriptures so that the message/lesson — i.e. God's Word — becomes written on your heart.

1. What has your prayer life been like?

2. Do you pray for small things, big things? Examples:

3. Has your prayer life changed for the better or worse over the years?

4. Do you pray with the belief that with God all things are possible? Can you find a scripture that states something like: "What is impossible to man is possible with God"?

5. Based on things you have learned thus far, how do you think your prayer life will be different now? Explain.

6. What point(s) resonated with you from this chapter? Describe. Incorporate scripture. The more you drench yourself in and with the Word, the more fortified in the faith you become.

Warrior Moms Unite! ™

Warrior Moms exposed the lies that I had been reciting in my head for years. Exchanging the lies for His truth literally changed my life. I now meditate on scripture more than ever and realize, through His Word and His strength, I can be a victorious Warrior Mom!

JULIE VanGILDER
WARRIOR MOM OF 2

www.WarriorMoms.net

CHAPTER 11

Please read the following chapter below from one of my other workbooks, *Corndogs by Candlelight*, about delegating responsibilities. It is essential that you understand this concept if you want to achieve balance in your heart and home.

Delegate

I remember reading about Moses' father-in-law telling him that he was trying to do too much by himself and that he should delegate some of the responsibility to other people:

Exodus 18:13-23   *The next day Moses took his seat to serve as judge for the people, and they stood around him from morning until evening. When his father-in-law saw all that Moses was doing for the people, he said, "What is this you are doing for the people? Why do you alone sit as judge, while all these people stand around you from morning until evening?" Moses answered him, "Because the people come to me to seek God's will. Whenever they have a dispute, it is brought to me, and I decide between the parties and inform them of God's decrees and laws." Moses' father-in-law replied, "What you are doing is not good. You and these people who come to you will only wear yourselves out. The work is too heavy for you; you cannot handle it alone. Listen to me and I will give you some advice, and may God be with you. You must be the people's representative before God and bring their disputes to him. Teach them the decrees and laws, and show them the way to live and the duties they are to perform. But select capable men from all the people – men who fear God, trustworthy men who hate dishonest gain – and appoint them as officials over thousands, hundreds, fifties and tens. Have them serve as judges for the people at all times, but have them bring every difficult case to you; the simple cases they can decide themselves. That will make your load lighter, because they will share it with you. If you do this and God so commands, you will be able to stand the strain, and all these people will go home satisfied."*

How does one copy Moses? You just do it! In the previous chapter, you identified some things that other people could do. So, you hold a family meeting, and you discuss the whole team thing, asking your family members to be a part of your team. When it comes to your kids, you instruct them as their mom and authority figure that they will have increased responsibilities in the house. Then you let them do their chores without nit-picking or telling them how they did it wrong.

If you are asking your 10 year old son to do laundry, you will first have to train him in that chore. You might even have to post the directions in the laundry room, but then you let him do it and let it go! So many moms don't want to let go of something because they want the dishwasher loaded a certain way, they want the towels folded a certain way, they want the bathroom cleaned a certain way. Give it up or you'll give yourself shingles!

If your mom was too critical of you, start to think about how you can be less critical of the people in your life. You can break the cycle because you have the power in Jesus Christ to do it. Philippians 4:13 says, *"I can do all things through him who gives me strength."*

YOU MUST TAKE TIME TO DELEGATE

Now, if you are married, when it comes to your husband, you can't just start bossing him around and yelling at him about how he's been a lazy, unappreciative bum for the last however many months or years. If you think about it for a minute, the reality is probably that you got married and just started doing everything like you were June Cleaver or something. Now that some time has passed, you're tired and you're wondering why your lazy husband isn't helping, when in reality you jumped into the marriage as Wonder Woman and now you are "Wondering Woman," wondering why your Clark Kent hasn't transformed into Superman himself!

Don't act self-righteous and start yelling and being mean about it. Did you ever do something for someone who first called you bad names? That approach doesn't work very well. How do politicians get votes? They know a lot about people. Politicians know that if they comprise a plan to meet the people's needs, those people are going to join their team because they know that they'll benefit from the politician's plan. And so the politician sets out to form relationships, goals, objectives, and results for the people.

It's the same for you. You must approach your husband in a nice, complimentary way and discuss your needs, the family's needs, his needs, and decide how together you can agree on goals and objectives.

If you are laughing out loud because your husband happens to idolize Fred Flintstone and he yells "WIIIIIIILLMMMAAAAAA" when he walks in the door, well, you're going to need more than what I just gave you. Remember that movie, *My Big Fat Greek Wedding*? Remember how the mom said something like the man may be the head of the household, but the woman controls the neck? Now, I'm not saying that you should be deceitful, but you know your husband best and you know how he responds to you. So, do your best to communicate with him. If it doesn't work, I might suggest marriage counseling. Most people wait until they're so mad and so discouraged that it's either marriage counseling or divorce. Don't wait that long. Do what you need to do now for the sake of your mental and physical health as well as for the sake of your team. Let me finish this chapter with my good friend, Fredda Harrison's, quote: "Take off those Super Woman tights, honey, and don't hang them on the shower curtain either – get rid of 'em!"

Exodus 18:22-23 *That will make your load lighter, because they will share it with you. If you do this and God so commands, you will be able to stand the strain, and all these people will go home satisfied.*

Evie, a Warrior Mom, made an additional point. She said that we must understand how to delegate so that we don't try to do it all by ourselves, leaving God out. God is willing and waiting to carry the burden of our load for us. Warrior Moms learn how to give it to God, relying on Him for strength, and trusting in Him for the outcome.

FIELD EXERCISES

Delegate one extra chore to each individual in the home. One of the original Warrior Moms decided that her children could do their own laundry. It revolutionized her life!

Husband's new chore(s): _____

Child 1's new chore: _____

Child 2's new chore: _____

Child 3's new chore: _____

Child 4's new chore: _____

Remember, they may not like it at first, but it will create more of a balance in your home. More importantly, you want to teach your children how to be servants so that before they go out into the world, they understand the value of serving rather than being served all the time. We don't want to send our children out into the world as if they are spoiled royalty who don't understand the gift of a servant-like heart. My 10 year old son does his own laundry also. Just think what a nice husband he'll be simply because he learned this concept early in life. I should back up — before he gets married, wearing clean clothes on a first date just might get him a second date.

MORE BRAINSTORMING REGARDING DELEGATION

_____
_____
_____
_____
_____
_____
_____
_____

Warrior Moms Unite! ™

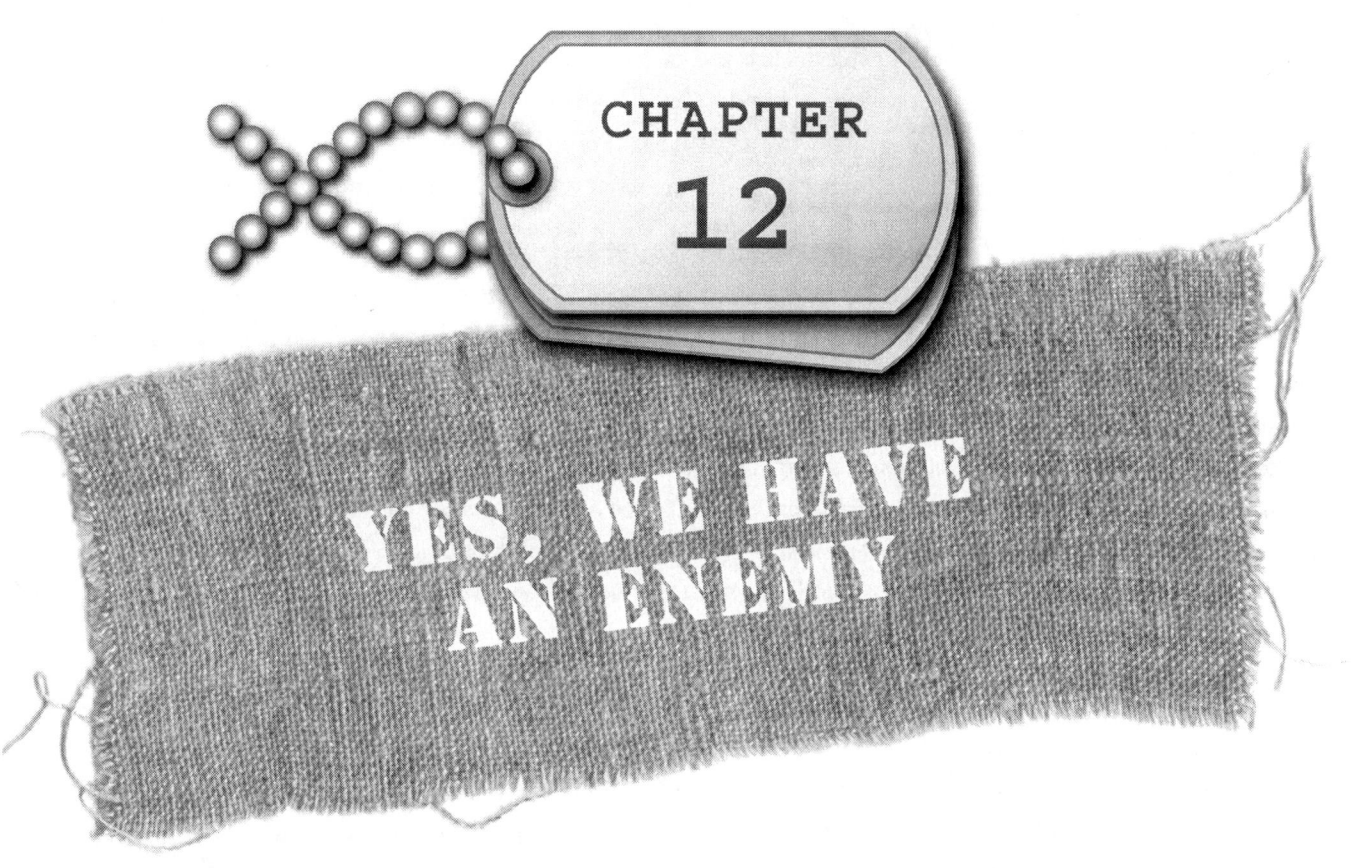

www.WarriorMoms.net

THE WARRIOR MOM HANDBOOK

Eventually, every soldier meets his opponent in battle. It's no different for the Warrior Mom. Remember Vietnam? Remember how the enemy used women and children to deceive the US soldiers? The enemy disguised themselves in the clothing of innocent women and children; their mission was to deceive. This was against the rules of war, but the enemy didn't care. Such is the case with our enemy. Think about this for a moment. The devil was cast out of heaven because he wanted to be as high and exalted as God, and he's been bent on destruction ever since. "Destruction against whom?" you ask. Let's look. Keep your pen or highlighter in hand. Underline things that reveal the enemy's tricks. Underline what you think is important to know about the enemy. Also, put a star next to things about the Lord that you learn as well.

Matthew 4:1-11   Then Jesus was led by the Spirit into the desert by the devil. After fasting forty days and forty nights, he was hungry. The tempter came to him and said, "If you are the Son of God, tell these stones to become bread." Jesus answered, "It is written: 'Man does not live on bread alone, but on every word that comes from the mouth of God.'" Then the devil took him to the holy city and had him stand on the highest point of the temple. "If you are the Son of God," he said, "throw yourself down. For it is written: "He will command his angels concerning you, and they will lift you up in their hands, so that you will not strike your foot against a stone."'" Jesus answered him, "It is also written: 'Do not put the Lord your God to the test.'" Again, the devil took him to a very high mountain and showed him all the kingdoms of the world and their splendor. "All this I will give you," he said, "if you will bow down and worship me." Jesus said to him, "Away from me, Satan! For it is written: 'Worship the Lord your God, and serve him only.'" Then the devil left him, and angels came and attended him.

Matthew 13:36-43   Then he left the crowd and went into the house. His disciples came to him and said, "Explain to us the parable of the weeds in the field." He answered, "The one who sowed the good seed is the Son of Man. The field is the world, and the good seed stands for the sons of the kingdom. The weeds are the sons of the evil one, and the enemy who sows them is the devil. The harvest is the end of the age, and the harvesters are angels. As the weeds are pulled up and burned in the fire, so it will be at the end of the age. The Son of Man will send out his angels, and they will weed out of his kingdom everything that causes sin and all who do evil. They will throw them into the fiery furnace, where there will be weeping and gnashing of teeth. The righteous will shine like the sun in the kingdom of their Father. He who has ears to hear let him hear."

Matthew 25:36-43   The King will reply, "I tell you the truth, whatever you did not do for one of the least of these, you did not do for me." Then they will go away to eternal punishment, but the righteous to eternal life. "Depart from me, you who are cursed, into the eternal fire prepared for the devil and his angels. For I was hungry and you gave me nothing to eat, I was thirsty and you gave me nothing to drink, I was a stranger and you did not invite me in, I needed clothes and you did not clothe me, I was sick and in prison and you did not look after me." They also will answer, "Lord, when did we see you hungry or thirsty or a stranger or needing clothes or sick or in prison, and did not help you?" He will reply, "I tell you the truth, whatever you did not do for one of the least of these, you did not do for me." Then they will go away to eternal punishment, but the righteous to eternal life.

Luke 4:1-13   Jesus, full of the Holy Spirit, returned from the Jordan and was led by the Spirit in the desert, where for forty days he was tempted by the devil. He ate nothing during those days, and at the end of them he was

YES, WE HAVE AN ENEMY

hungry. The devil said to him, "If you are the Son of God, tell this stone to become bread." Jesus answered, "It is written; 'Man does not live on bread alone.'" The devil led him up to a high place and showed him in an instant all the kingdoms of the world. And he said to him, "I will give you all their authority and splendor, for it has been given to me, and I can give it to anyone I want. So if you worship me, it will all be yours." Jesus answered, "It is written: 'Worship the Lord your God and serve him only.'" The devil led him to Jerusalem and had him stand on the highest point of the temple. "If you are the Son of God," he said, "throw yourself down from here. For it is written: 'He will command his angels concerning you to guard you carefully; they will lift you up in their hands, so that you will not strike your foot against a stone.'" Jesus answered, "It says: 'Do not put the Lord your God to the test.'" When the devil had finished all of this tempting, he left him until an opportune time.

Luke 8:11-15 This is the meaning of the parable: The seed is the word of God. Those along the path are the ones who hear, and then the devil comes and takes away the word from their hearts, so that they may not believe and be saved. Those on the rock are the ones who receive the word with joy when they hear it, but they have no root. They believe for a while, but in the time of testing they fall away. The seed that fell among thorns stands for those who hear, but as they go on their way they are choked by life's worries, riches and pleasures, and they do not mature. But the seed on good soil stands for those with a noble and good heart, who hear the word, retain it, and by persevering produce a crop.

John 6:70 Then Jesus replied, "Have I not chosen you, the Twelve? Yet one of you is a devil!" (He meant Judas, the son of Simon Iscariot, who though one of the Twelve, was later to betray him.)

John 8:42-47 Jesus said to them, "If God were your Father, you would love me, for I came from God and now am here. I have not come on my own; but he sent me. Why is my language not clear to you? Because you are unable to hear what I say. You belong to your father, the devil, and you want to carry out your father's desire. He was a murderer from the beginning, not holding the truth, for there is no truth in him. When he lies, he speaks his native language, for he is a liar and the father of lies. Yet because I tell the truth, you do not believe me! Can any of you prove me guilty of sin? If I am telling the truth, why don't you believe me? He who belongs to God hears what God says. The reason you do not hear is that you do not belong to God."

John 13:2 The evening meal was being served, and the devil had already prompted Judas Iscariot, son of Simon, to betray Jesus. Jesus knew that the Father had put all things under his power, and that he had come from God and was returning to God.

Acts 10:34-38 Then Peter began to speak: "I now realize how true it is that God does not show favoritism but accepts men from every nation who fear him and do what is right. You know the message of God sent to the people of Israel, telling the good news of peace through Jesus Christ, who is Lord of all. You know what has happened throughout Judea, beginning in Galilee after the baptism that John preached—how God anointed Jesus of Nazareth with the Holy Spirit and power, and how he went around doing good and healing all who were under the power of the devil, because God was with him."

Acts 13:9-11 Then Saul, who was also called Paul, filled with the Holy Spirit, looked straight at Elymas (a sorcerer) and said, "You are a child of the devil and an enemy of everything that is right! You are full of all kinds of deceit and trickery. Will you never stop perverting the right ways of the Lord? Now the hand of the Lord is against you. You are going to be blind, and for a time you will be unable to see the light of the sun."

Ephesians 4:25-28   Therefore each of you must put off falsehood and speak truthfully to his neighbor, for we are all members of one body. "In your anger do not sin." Do not let the sun go down while you are still angry, and do not give the devil a foothold. He who has been stealing must steal no longer, but must work, doing something useful with his own hands, that he may have something to share with those in need.

I Timothy 3:6   He must not be a recent convert, or he may become conceited and fall under the same judgment as the devil.

II Timothy 2:24-26   And the Lord's servant must not quarrel; instead, he must be kind to everyone, able to teach, not resentful. Those who oppose him he must gently instruct, in the hope that God will grant them repentance leading them to a knowledge of the truth, and they will come to their senses and escape from the trap of the devil, who has taken them captive to do his will.

Hebrews 2:14-18   Since the children have flesh and blood, he too shared in their humanity so that by his death he might destroy him who holds the power of death – that is, the devil – and free those who all their lives were held in slavery by their fear of death. For surely it is not angels he helps, but Abraham's descendants. For this reason he had to be made like his brothers in every way, in order that he might become a merciful and faithful high priest in service to God, and that he might make atonement for the sins of the people. Because he himself suffered when he was tempted, he is able to help those who are being tempted.

James 3:13-16   Who is wise and understanding among you? Let him show it by his good life, by deeds done in the humility that comes from wisdom. But if you harbor bitter envy and selfish ambition in your hearts, do not boast about it or deny the truth. Such wisdom does not come down from heaven but is earthly, unspiritual, of the devil. For where you have envy and selfish ambition, there you find disorder and every evil practice.

James 4:7-8   Submit yourselves, then, to God. Resist the devil, and he will flee from you. Come near to God and he will come near to you.

I Peter 5:8-11   Be self-controlled and alert. Your enemy the devil prowls around like a roaring lion looking for someone to devour. Resist him, standing firm in the faith, because you know that your brothers throughout the world are undergoing the same kind of sufferings. And the God of grace, who called you to his eternal glory in Christ, after you have suffered a little while, will himself restore you and make you strong, firm and steadfast. To him be the power forever and ever. Amen.

I John 3:7-10   Dear children, do not let anyone lead you astray. He who does what is right is righteous, just as he is righteous. He who does what is sinful is of the devil, because the devil has been sinning from the beginning. The reason the Son of God appeared was to destroy the devil's work. No one who is born of God will continue to sin, because God's seed remains in him; he cannot go on sinning, because he has been born of God. This is how we know who the children of God are and who the children of the devil are: Anyone who does not do what is right is not a child of God; nor is anyone who does not love his brother.

YES, WE HAVE AN EMEMY

Jude 1:8-10   In the very same way, these dreamers pollute their own bodies, reject authority and slander celestial beings. But even the archangel Michael, when he was disputing with the devil about the body of Moses, did not dare to bring a slanderous accusation against him, but said, "The Lord rebuke you!" Yet these men speak abusively against whatever they do not understand; and what things they do understand by instinct, like unreasoning animals – these are the very things that destroy them.

Revelation 2:8-11   "These are the words of him who is the First and the Last, who died and came to life again. I know your afflictions and your poverty – yet you are rich! I know the slander of those who say they are Jews and are not, but are a synagogue of Satan. Do not be afraid of what you are about to suffer. I tell you, the devil will put some of you in prison to test you, and you will suffer persecution for ten days. Be faithful, even to the point of death, and I will give you the crown of life. He who has an ear, let him hear what the Spirit says to the churches. He who overcomes will not be hurt at all by the second death."

Warrior Moms, really listen to this next one — it speaks to Warrior Moms.

Revelation 12:7-17,13:1   And there was a war in heaven. Michael and his angels fought against the dragon, and the dragon and his angels fought back. But he was not strong enough, and they lost their place in heaven. The great dragon was hurled down–the ancient serpent called the devil, or Satan, who leads the whole world astray. He was hurled to the earth, and his angels with him. Then I heard a voice in heaven say: "Now have come the salvation and the power and the kingdom of our God, and the authority of his Christ. For the accuser of our brothers, who accuses them before our God day and night, has been hurled down. They overcame him by the blood of the Lamb and by the word of their testimony; they did not love their lives so much as to shrink from death. Therefore rejoice, you heavens and you who dwell in them! But woe to the earth and the sea, because the devil has gone down to you! He is filled with fury, because he knows that his time is short." When the dragon saw that he had been hurled to the earth, he pursued the woman who had given birth to the male child. The woman was given the two wings of a great eagle, so that she might fly to the place prepared for her in the desert, where she would be taken care of for a time, times and half a time, out of the serpent's reach. Then from his mouth the serpent spewed water like a river, to overtake the woman and sweep her away with the torrent. But the earth helped the woman by opening its mouth and swallowing the river that the dragon had spewed out of his mouth. Then the dragon was enraged at the woman and went off to make war against the rest of her offspring–those who obey God's commandments and hold to the testimony of Jesus. And the dragon stood at the shore of the sea.

Revelation 20:1-10   Then I saw an angel coming down out of heaven, having the key to the Abyss and holding in his hand a great chain. He seized the dragon, the ancient serpent, who is the devil, or Satan, and bound him for a thousand years. He threw him into the Abyss, and locked and sealed it over him, to keep him from deceiving the nations anymore until the thousand years were ended. After that, he must be set free for a short time. I saw thrones on which were seated those who had been given authority to judge. And I saw the souls of those who had been beheaded because of their testimony for Jesus and because of the word of God. They had not worshiped the beast or his image and had not received his mark on their foreheads or their hands. They came to life and reigned with Christ a thousand years. (The rest of the dead did not come to life until the thousand years were ended.) This is the first resurrection. Blessed and holy are those who have part in the first resurrection. The second death has no power over them, but they will be priests of God and of Christ and will reign with him for a thousand years.

When the thousand years were over, Satan will be released from his prison and will go out to deceive the nations in the four corners of the earth–Gog and Magog–to gather them for battle. In number they are like the sand of the seashore. They marched across the breadth of the earth and surrounded the camp of God's people, the city he loves. But fire came down from heaven and devoured them. The devil who deceived them, was thrown into the lake of burning sulfur, where the beast and the false prophet had been thrown. They will be tormented day and night forever and ever.

Ephesians 6:10-11   *Finally, be strong in the Lord and in his mighty power. Put on the full armor of God so that you can take your stand against the devil's schemes.*

I Timothy 3:7   *He must also have a good reputation with outsiders, so that he will not fall into disgrace and into the devil's trap.*

Wow! Okay, ready? I noticed quite a bit. Compare your notes with mine. Add new ones that I may have missed.

1. The enemy dares you to prove yourself. God accepts us. We don't have to and we can't impress our way into heaven. He tempted Jesus to prove that He was the Son of God. Jesus doesn't owe Satan proof that He is who He is, and as daughters to the King, nor do we! Don't fall for senseless dares.

   _____
   _____

2. When you notice a weed, know it is from the enemy. Weeds take many forms: gossip, slander, deceit, jealousy, inferiority, shame, guilt, condemnation, lust, coveting, and/or people you shouldn't hang out with because they constantly tempt you to evil rather than lift up the Lord while offering you support. Name your weeds; don't be deceived!

   _____
   _____

3. When God taps you on the shoulder or winks at you by placing people who are hungry, thirsty, in prison, or unclothed in front of you, obey and give to them. No, you can't save the world. Jesus already did that. And Jesus doesn't expect you to be Him and save the world. When Mother Teresa was asked, "How do you—one woman—expect to solve world hunger?" she replied, "One mouth at a time." And so, when God sends you an assignment, salute and do it.

   _____
   _____

4. The devil does flee, but he returns at another opportune time. And I will guarantee you, it will be a moment in which you forgot to put on your armor, and it will be in your spiritual blind spot. Additionally, it will probably be in reference to a familiar weed or weakness of yours. Be alert!

   _____
   _____

YES, WE HAVE AN EMEMY

5. The devil seeks to steal the Word from your heart to keep you from believing. He does this with lies of doubt and condemnation. He figures if he can make you feel bad enough, you won't stay in the Word with your focus on God. This allows you to be vulnerable to his kicks. With no armor on, kicks hurt. With armor on, the one who kicks gets hurt. He'll try to yell hate and hopelessness into your ears. Sing praises to God louder! Have you ever noticed that once you whisper or think a negative sentence of despair, it multiplies in half a second?! And suddenly you're crying, eating chocolate, and not answering calls from your best friend?! Am I the only one who has done that? I think I could find someone else who would admit that she's been there also.

    _____
    _____
    _____
    _____

6. Satan wants you to betray your faith. Once you are saved, you can hear God in many ways. It might be through gentle nudges to help someone. Your conscience doesn't allow you to give into sin like before. You see beauty in God's creation. You begin to appreciate His grace in your life, in your spouse, your children, and your friends. You begin to see His love all around in ways you never saw before. These are your eyes of faith. Little "God" things happen that you can't explain. Yes, that's God your heart is hearing and you know it's Him. If you don't feel that you've ever heard from God, ask Him to speak to you in a way that only you and He knows about. When He speaks, you'll know it's Him. Satan wants you to think faith is silly. He wants you to think that the things you are hearing and seeing from God are just your wild imagination. He lives to lie to you.

    _____
    _____
    _____
    _____

7. People who constantly seek evil are from the evil one. Learn to discern and protect yourself from the enemy's attempt to pull you into his den. The enemy prompts his evil sons and daughters to plot against us. Sure, our battle is not with flesh and blood, but that doesn't mean the enemy won't use flesh and blood to get to us. It's one of his best tools — people! Focusing on people keeps us from realizing that it's a spiritual battle that's going on. Be alert and remind yourself that it's not the person or circumstance in front of you that you battle, it's the enemy that you battle. And who has already won? Jesus. So say, "Game over!" and don't be full of fear but be full of faith!

    _____
    _____

8. P.S., God doesn't play favorites. So, when the enemy says, "*Why would God care for you, you of all people, who are you anyway?*" Say, "*God does not show favoritism but accepts men from every nation who fear him and do what is right!*" (Acts 10:34) And then add: "*Greater is he that is in me than he that is in the world.*" (I John 4:4)

_____

_____

_____

9. The devil gets a foothold when you go to bed angry.

_____

_____

10. The devil is conceited and wants you to be conceited also. What may you be conceited about? It's a trap. We should only brag in/on Christ and His power.

_____

_____

11. When you quarrel and are resentful, the enemy is smiling. Be alert!

_____

_____

12. The enemy uses slavery and fear of death to scare you. The enemy loves to keep you in that mindset. If you are saved, death can't hold you. To be absent from the body is to be present with Christ (II Corinthians 5:6). Jesus died once and for all. Being held as a slave to death is to live in a lie. If you are not saved, you can be saved by asking forgiveness for your sins, professing Jesus as the Son of God, and asking Him into your heart as your Lord and Savior. If you just did that, it's a done deal, and you are saved. Let your leader know you are saved so she can support you on your new walk with the Lord.

_____

_____

13. When you feel all alone, like no one gets it or cares, it's a lie. Jesus has been there, done that, and He knows and He cares for you.

_____

_____

14. The enemy loves to spread selfish ambition. Wherever it is, the enemy dances. Resist!

_____

_____

15. The enemy is looking for weak, unprotected children. He desires to eat you up and spit you out.
_____
_____

16. The devil is constantly trying to lead you astray.
_____
_____

17. **A Very Important Point!**

Do not say a slanderous word to the enemy. (Please highlight this in your handbook.) Not even the archangel, Michael, did so. Remember, the enemy wants you to fight with him so that he can prove himself and unleash on you. Therefore, stand firm in the Word, but don't say a slanderous word. Not even Jesus did such a thing! Don't get puffed up and say something to the enemy that he's waiting for the chance to pounce on. Do not say a slanderous word. I can't stress this enough. Don't even brag in your strength as a warrior! This is extremely dangerous territory my friend. No "Oh yeah..." type statements. I learned this the hard way, after I got all puffed up in my warriorness. I was nearly swallowed whole, along with my family; torn to shreds is a better description. Write this one down on an index card, memorize it. Remember that other index card about praying for protection? Praying for protection is wise, whereas saying a slanderous word to the enemy is extremely dangerous.

Also, remember the lesson from Chapter 10, and do not engage in hour-long (or decade long) debates with the enemy. He usually keeps people busy arguing about whether or not they are worthy, but he may have picked a new topic, specific to you, with which to argue. Beware! He is using the Word against you if all you are doing is defending yourself with the Word. Rather than marching forward in victory, accomplishing work for the Kingdom, he's gotten you to chase your tail and defend yourself. God intends for us to march forward in unity, linked together, as a powerful Army - The Body of Christ. Instead, many Christians find themselves detached from the Body, defending themselves alone, and all the while they think they are being victorious because they are using the Word in their defense. The enemy is a master of deception; he considers it a major victory if he merely separates you from the platoon and takes you off course into the jungle land of confusing debates. So, whenever you find yourself arguing for more than five minutes with the enemy, an alarm should go off within your soul. Stop. Press into the Word, ignore the enemy, link back up with the platoon, and press onward to victory. Forward, march!
_____
_____
_____

18. The devil loves to put you in prison and persecute you. Make sure you don't help him build the prison of depression and despair by laying there while he puts brick on top of brick. Whose side are you on, Warrior Mom?! See how he deceives? He even gets you to work with him against yourself. Remember the Lucy and Ethel skit at the beginning of the handbook? No more! Hear you roar!

_____

_____

_____

_____

19. And finally, at the end of this lesson, we find out why the devil has such a (rib) bone to pick with us women and our offspring. You've heard about the war on the family, right? Well, Revelation 12:7-17 explains it perfectly. Read that one again. As I reflect on this profound discovery (I know others have discussed it, but I just found it out for myself through this long study on the enemy), I have learned that there was a battle against me. I could feel that a new truth and a new power were going to be discovered. Take note of such events. When you feel sad, depressed, like you have no energy and you can't figure out what's going on with you, think about it and say, "Aha! ==Something great is about to happen or be revealed! I must persevere and ask God to fight for me, to give me His strength, and I must believe and have faith — I must!==" And when the waves of the storm become calm, you will see with clarity what was at stake. A truth will be revealed or a breakthrough will occur in communication with your spouse, your child, your boss, your husband's boss, your kid's math lesson, a teacher, or a soul gets saved. Whatever it is that was at stake will be revealed after the battle has been won. If you give up beforehand, you'll never know what was at stake; you'll only suffer the unknown losses. More importantly, blessings are coming that you can't even fathom! And so you must persevere! Things are at stake that you don't even know about yet. You must be alert to notice when you are under attack, and you must fight back in faith.

Wear the armor. Quote scripture. Praise God. Claim victory and say, "Okay, I feel bad, weak, unable — but my God is my strength and my song! My God will deliver me. Those who hope in the Lord will not be disappointed! I do not trust in circumstances or people. I will cast out doubt. Greater is He that is in me than he that is in the world!"

In fact, next time things are really bad, your eyebrows should go up as you say, "Aha! This is my sign, my red flag. This is a reminder that the game is on, but the glory of God will be revealed." Then, buckle up and hold on. Surround yourself with other Warrior Moms and pray. Praise God through the storm. Then shield your eyes with a Son-visor to protect yourself from the bright, glorious light that is about to break through your darkness. Something great is about to happen; that's why you are under attack! Fight back in faith!

YES, WE HAVE AN ENEMY

It makes sense that Satan is after women. After all, a woman bore Jesus, and women keep providing additional future saints for God's Army. And if the enemy can defeat women, he can defeat all who are in their homes. It's like a four-for-one deal for him. He thinks, "If I can get the mom, the others will be that much easier to take." See?! You set the warrior tone for your home, and you are either a warrior who is raising warriors and encouraging your husband in the Word or you aren't. If you are a warrior, your home and all the souls in it are growing more and more fortified in the faith! See what is at stake here? Sure, many things, but ultimately we are talking about souls. The battle is not against flesh and blood — it's not.

_____
_____
_____
_____
_____

20. Oh, and the devil knows his time is short. Just remind him of that! Quote the verse. Read it out loud and he will flee. It's like this: a bully on the playground only picks on those that allow themselves to be victims. But, if the little kid who has been picked on for years says, "No more! No more lies. No more stealing my lunch money (or joy)! No more calling me 'nerd,' no more!" And, if the kid learns karate and kicks the bully's tail, well, the bully will flee. Don't say these things to the enemy; I use them here as samples of a bully on a playground, not so you can use it as a script. Remember, not a slanderous word.

The same is true for us. Don't fear the enemy. He lies to you to get you defeated and make you think he's bigger and stronger than you. Once he convinces you of that lie, he continues to kick you while you're down. He wants to make sure that you never look up to God for God's strength. Well, we just flipped over the rock under which he was hiding, and now you know who your enemy is. You also know his strategies. Don't be deceived by the form in which he appears. Don't be surprised by his tactics. Remember Vietnam? Rise up, Warrior Mom! You've got the power of Jesus Christ in you! The enemy must flee. Sure, he'll be back, but you'll be ready, not to be attacked but to defend yourself with the Word of God. Victors in Jesus Christ don't let bullies intimidate them.

_____
_____
_____
_____
_____

FIELD EXERCISES

Review and reflect upon these verses.

1. What is a very important element regarding the enemy that you have learned?
   (Please write down that you now know not to say a slanderous word as a reminder), but then record more insights you have gained.

   _____
   _____
   _____
   _____

2. What is an important lesson that you have realized about Jesus and how He handled the enemy? (This may be a difficult question. If you can't think of an answer, don't worry, we'll discuss it in more depth in the next chapter, but I'm interested if you noticed anything regarding how Jesus responded to the enemy?)

   _____
   _____
   _____
   _____

3. In what areas of your life has the enemy gotten a foothold? More than likely, there's a repeated issue in your life, a repeated weakness of some sort. Insecurity, anger, resentment, fear of (fill in the blank.) How do I know this? Because we are all human, and we all have our own baggage we carry around. The enemy uses that baggage. How freeing does it sound to look at that baggage from a spiritual perspective rather than a physical perspective? Doesn't it become a little lighter? I want you to list these weaknesses. You may have one particular weakness that you can think of; you may have twenty. List as many as you can. You must be aware that the enemy uses these things against you. You must be aware of these weaknesses and use them as red-flagged areas that you can entrust to God to help you grow, rather than let the enemy use them as bullets against you.

   _____
   _____
   _____
   _____
   _____

Warrior Moms Unite! ™

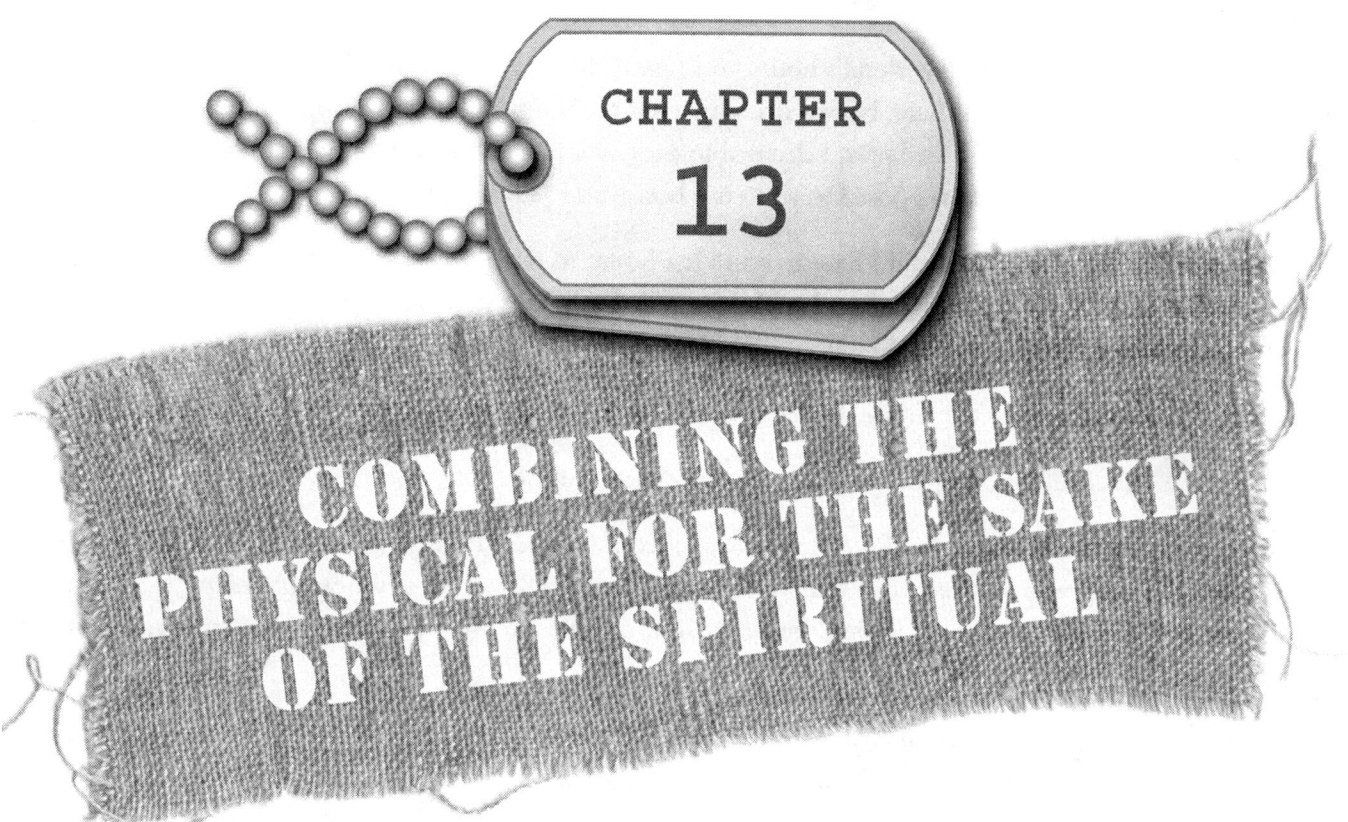

CHAPTER 13

COMBINING THE PHYSICAL FOR THE SAKE OF THE SPIRITUAL

www.WarriorMoms.net

CHAPTER 13

Think about the weaknesses you listed in the previous chapter in more of a spiritual sense than in a physical sense. It is important to know that the spiritual and the physical are important, and they can work together for your good or for your defeat. Let me explain.

One day, God told me to go to my friend's house and pray. I thought, " Okay, I will." But, when I got there, nobody was home. Her car was there, but no one answered the door. Thinking this odd, but knowing that God told me to go to her house and pray, I decided to pray over her house and for her family without her. Originally, I assumed that I was supposed to go to her house and pray with her.

Driving away, I asked God, "Why did I have to go to her house to pray? She wasn't there, and I could have prayed for her while I was driving or when I got home. We don't have to be physically present somewhere to pray for someone or for something, do we?"

God said, "When you combine the physical for the sake of the spiritual, the spiritual becomes that much stronger."

"Oh, I get it," I replied. "Yes, they do that time and time again in the Bible, don't they?"

Yes, there were instances where people marched and circled Jericho, *"By faith the walls of Jericho fell, after the people marched around them for seven days."* (Hebrews 11:30) Another instance of combining the physical for the sake of the spiritual comes to mind as well. It was when men held up Moses' arms to defeat the Amalekites.

Exodus 17:8-13   *The Amalekites came and attacked the Israelites at Rephidim. Moses said to Joshua, "Choose some of our men and go out to fight the Amalekites. Tomorrow I will stand on top of the hill with the staff of God in my hands." So, Joshua fought the Amalekites as Moses had ordered, and Moses, Aaron and Hur went to the top of the hill.*

As long as Moses held up his hands, the Israelites were winning, but whenever he lowered his hands, the Amalekites were winning. When Moses' hands grew tired, they took a stone and put it under him and he sat on it. Aaron and Hur held his hands up-one on one side, one on the other-so that his hands remained steady till sunset. So Joshua overcame the Amalekite army with the sword.

It was a physical battle, but through Moses' faith, and by Moses combining the physical raising of his hands for the sake of the spiritual, they received victory. But the supreme example of combining the physical for the sake of the spiritual is Jesus' sacrifice on the cross.

Colossians 1:13-20   *For he has rescued us from the dominion of darkness and brought us into the kingdom of the Son he loves, in whom we have redemption, the forgiveness of sins. He is the image of the invisible God, the firstborn over all creation. For by him all things were created: things in heaven and on earth, visible and invisible, whether thrones or powers or rulers or authorities; all things were created by him and for him. He is before all things, and in him all things hold together. And he is the head of the body, the church; he is the beginning and the firstborn from among the dead, so that in everything he might have supremacy. For God was pleased to have all his fullness dwell in him, and through him to reconcile to himself all things, whether things on earth or things in heaven, by making peace through his blood, shed on the cross.*

COMBINING THE PHYSICAL FOR THE SAKE OF THE SPIRITUAL

And the example of Jesus is supreme because while He was on this earth, He battled the physical with the spiritual. And at the end, He shed the physical body He wore while He was here. He died for us, paying the ultimate price for our sins so that we might receive His gift of eternal life. We can see the big picture in this: that if we receive His gift we will receive eternal life. But what about after we get saved? What about our days on this earth? What are we to do with those? To win the battles and to win the all-out wars against us, we must do as Jesus did. ==We must die to self.==

Romans 14:7-10 *For none of us lives to himself alone and none of us dies to himself alone. If we live, we live to the Lord; and if we die, we die to the Lord. So, whether we live or die, we belong to the Lord. For this very reason, Christ died and returned to life so that he might be the Lord of both the dead and the living. You then, why do you judge your brother? Or why do you look down on your brother? For we will all stand before God's judgment seat.*

I Corinthians 15:31-32 *I die every day, I mean that brothers – just as surely as I glory over you in Christ Jesus our Lord. If I fought wild beasts in Ephesus for merely human reasons, what have I gained?*

Philippians 1:19-21 *Yes, and I will continue to rejoice, for I know that through your prayers and the help given by the Spirit of Jesus Christ, what has happened to me will turn out for my deliverance. I eagerly expect and hope that I will in no way be ashamed, but will have sufficient courage so that now as always Christ will be exalted in my body, whether by life or by death. For to me, to live is Christ and to die is gain.*

I Peter 2:23-25 *When they hurled their insults at him, he did not retaliate; when he suffered, he made no threats. Instead he entrusted himself to him who judges justly. He himself bore our sins in his body on the tree, so that we might die to sins and live for righteousness; by his wounds you have been healed. For you were like sheep going astray, but now you have returned to the Shepherd and Overseer of your souls.*

Just as all great lessons require hands-on experience, so too it is with life. Recently, I was nuked by the enemy. It was right after I wrote that last chapter warning everyone about such an event. Of course, that makes sense. After all, I committed to write this Warrior Mom study, so it made sense that the enemy was after me. However, I didn't realize that I would receive a hands-on tutorial of what I was writing about.

As I mentioned earlier, the enemy attacks at your weak points. What I learned later is that he always plans a nuclear attack once he's worn you down a little. First he tried to get at me through one of my known weaknesses. Though that hurt, it didn't work. I quoted scripture, I praised God, and I claimed victory. Second, he tried to get at me through my offspring. I said, "Aha, you won't get at me through my child!" I did the same thing. I quoted scripture, praised God, and claimed victory. But my mistake was in thinking that the coast was clear after all that. I recently learned that the nuclear attack comes after a few little battles. Sure, we don't think they are little at the time. They are exhausting and gut-wrenching so how can they be little? Trust me, they are little compared to what he's up to. So, what did I learn? When the little battles start, and I realize that I'm being attacked, I gear up more! I call in support prayer warriors and really seek the spiritual.

The final nuclear attack was horrible. I was unjustly accused and my heart was crushed. I tried to state my case to the one I loved, but I wasn't heard. I was flabbergasted that the one I loved didn't hear me or understand. In fact, I was attacked by my loved one even more, and my life and family were threatened! I found myself on the floor completely empty, depleted, done! I actually felt a physical force on my arms. Some might call it depression — you know how your limbs are so heavy they can't move? It was a strong force, and I felt it pushing my arms into my sides, down into my stomach. I could barely lift them, let alone my eyes to the Lord. But I cried out.

I called fellow Warrior Moms. We discovered something. In a nutshell, I had to quit fighting in the physical. I had to quit stating my case to my loved one. It was a trick. My loved one's ears were deaf to my case and the more I tried to justify my pain to gain understanding, the further the divide between us grew. Fellow Warrior Moms agreed with me. It was official: what was being done to me was wrong. So, in the flesh everyone agreed with my side. But that didn't matter. I had to let it go. The fact that I was justified, that I was right, and that what was being done to me was wrong, well, all that was reason enough to stick to my guns. But, it was a trick of the enemy! The enemy wanted me to stick my heels in the ground and stick to my justification and rightness in this matter. He was nuking me with my own justification, rightness, pain, and need to be heard. It was at that moment that a light bulb went off. The only way to win this war was to quit fighting, and to quit stating my case to my loved one. It was like a revelation to me. So, I nailed it to the cross. I stopped fighting. I asked for forgiveness for what my loved one felt that I had done.

No, I was never heard by my loved one. I still am not heard today, but God hears my cry. God knows, and God understands. More importantly, I learned that the enemy was trying to get me to fight for my right to be heard. He is constantly trying to use us against ourselves! It's a smart tactic on his part. If he puts us on autopilot against ourselves, he is free to go pick on someone else. In my mind, I had a perfectly good right reason to support my cause. But hear me loud and clear, had I kept pushing and fighting for my right to be heard, I would have been destroyed. Our family would have been ripped to shreds! That is what the enemy is after. He wants to blind you and get you to fight your own battles based on heartaches, justice, emotion, and simply being right. It's not worth it! It's a trick! It's the nuke! I want you to get this in your core.

Learn to recognize the little battles and expect a nuclear attack. If you don't train yourself in this way, you will succumb to the nuclear attack and you will lose, your husband will lose, and your children will lose. You have to learn to notice the warning signs and wear the armor.

COMBINING THE PHYSICAL FOR THE SAKE OF THE SPIRITUAL

Example:
1. Someone attacks your character.
2. Someone attacks your child in some way.
3. Someone attacks your finances.
4. Your car breaks down.
5. You begin fighting with your spouse over one or all of these issues.
6. Your husband doesn't hear you; he even says "You're nuts!"
7. You wonder, "What's going on around here?!"
8. You realize you are under attack.
9. You expect a nuclear attack and you prepare for it!
10. You don't fight back in emotion or in seeking your own right to be heard. You realize that this battle is not against flesh and blood, and you stop the enemy in his tracks!

The hard part is that once you are worn down and a little dizzy, you might be blind to the fact that this is spiritual, not physical. You might think, "This is all about me, my pain, my hurt, my child's pain, my child's hurt, etc." No, it's not! This is about the enemy trying to wear you down so he can really unleash on you. Once a soldier has taken a bullet in the shin and suffered a few cuts to his good arm, it's harder to fight. It's then that the fight really starts. You must get this or you will fight great little battles, but you will lose nuclear war after nuclear war. This refers to shedding the physical self. You must die to self. It is only when you completely die to self that God is able to win wars for you. Read that last sentence a couple of times.

I suggest that we all carry a little nail around with us as a reminder that we must nail the issues to the cross. We must nail the little battles to the cross, as well as prepare ourselves to think in sacrificial ways. We must do this because we now know that once little battles start, we can expect a nuclear attack. How do you know when to pull the nail out and nail yourself to the cross? You pray for God to tell you, and usually it's at that critical moment when it has escalated to a high point and you're wondering, "What is going on around here?" It's at that moment that you pull out the nail and prepare to nail yourself to the cross so that you can shed the physical and receive the spiritual victory! Don't be fooled, Warrior Moms. Be prepared! Got nails?

The Lord is my strength and my song; he has become my salvation. He is my God, and I will praise him; my father's God, and I will exalt him. The Lord is a warrior; the Lord is his name. (Exodus 15:2-3)

Some Warrior Moms in the first class asked, "Does this mean we are to just let people walk all over us?" By no means do I mean that! Does it mean that being loving and humble are the way to go? Yes. Each situation that you will face will be unique to you, so what I suggest is that you seek God before you respond, always. I learned the hard way that since I was not being heard, the only way for me to win in that situation was to sacrifice and give up my right to be right (and my desire to be heard). Now, was my life at stake? No. My pride and my broken heart were at stake, but there's a big difference between danger and pride. And don't forget, there are times when we must do as Jesus did and get angry and turn over the tables (John 2:15). But if you want answers as to when you are supposed to turn over a table, go to God and ask Him. There are countless times in the Bible where Jesus was loving and humble, and only one time where He turned over a table. I want to follow His lead regarding this issue.

FIELD EXERCISES

1. Write down an instance where battles came and then a nuke followed.
   _____
   _____
   _____
   _____

2. Do you have a better understanding of how the enemy works? Please describe.
   _____
   _____
   _____
   _____

3. What are some things that you can do differently now that you know how the enemy works?
   _____
   _____
   _____
   _____

4. Review Jesus' prayer in Matthew 6. Write it out and begin to memorize it.
   _____
   _____
   _____
   _____

5. With your new insights regarding the enemy, what are your thoughts regarding praying for protection?
   _____
   _____
   _____
   _____

Warrior Moms Unite! ™

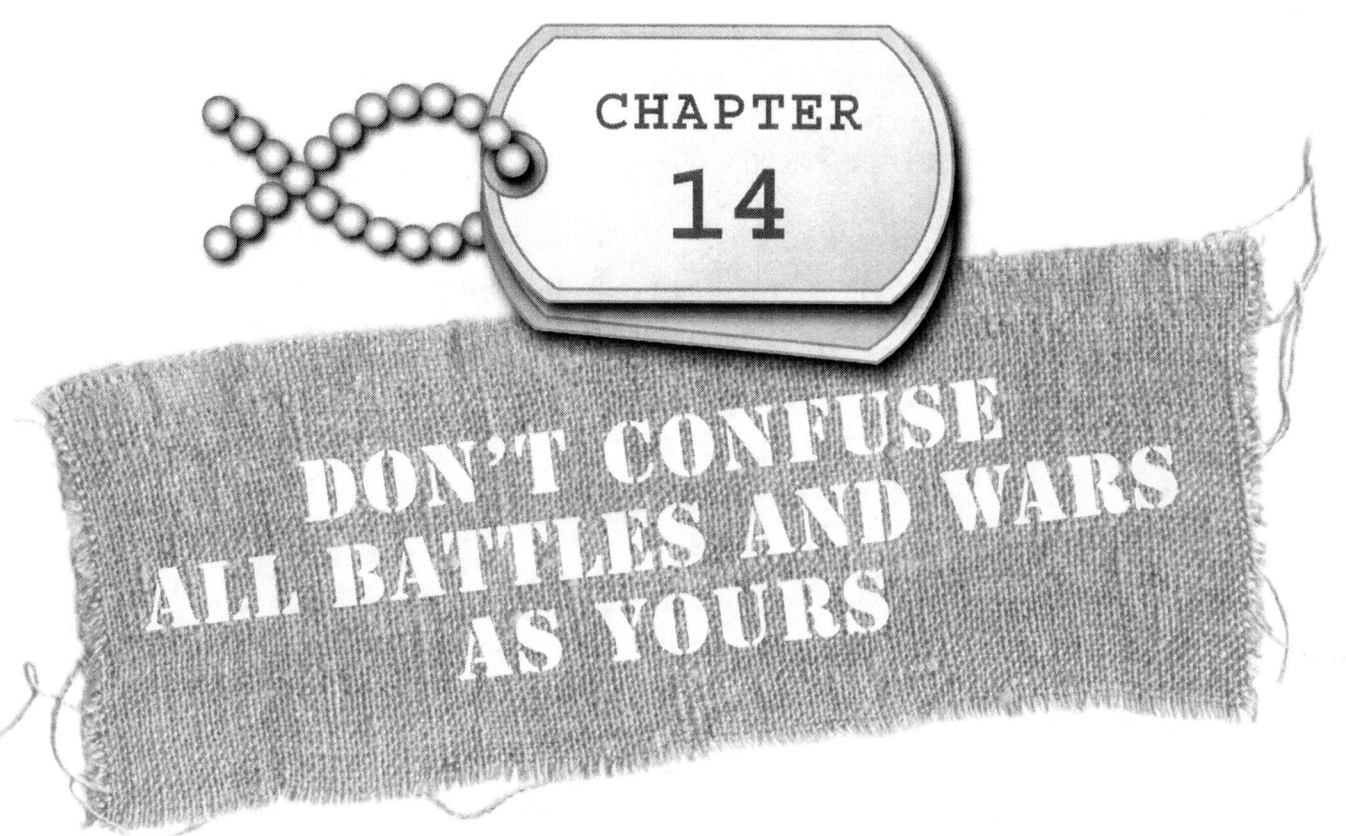

www.WarriorMoms.net

CHAPTER 14

I almost wrote a handbook leading many women into an ambush. God let me experience an ambush so that I would learn a valuable lesson for the sake of all Warrior Moms everywhere. Don't confuse all battles and all wars in existence with the ones that are yours. You might want to underline, highlight, and memorize that sentence. In a nutshell, your battles are the ones that God has allowed to come your way. You deal with the wars that God allows in your path. Yes, you battle, and you do all the things you've learned in this handbook. You fight the good fight, and you pull out that nail and remember that the way to really win a war is through sacrifice. Jesus is our supreme example of that. But you never go seeking battles and wars with the enemy.

How did I learn that the hard way, you ask? Well, right before I got nuked in the last chapter, I was talking with God about all my battles. I was asking God to take my thoughts captive and speak to me. My thoughts were not serving me well. I was really struggling with the physical, and while I knew all the stuff in this handbook, it didn't make it any easier. When you are experiencing physical pain and emotional trials/personal junk, it's difficult! There's no other way to say it. It's difficult. So, I was asking God to take my thoughts captive and to speak to me.

The first day, God said, *"This is a test."*

I said, "Isn't all of life a test?!" God knew I wasn't trying to be rude, but He knew that I was struggling. That's all He said to me that day. I focused on the fact that this was just a test, and I did all I knew to do:

1. I quoted scripture.
2. I praised God. *"Through Jesus, therefore, let us continually offer to God a sacrifice of praise – the fruit of the lips that confess his name."* (Hebrews 13:15)
3. I resisted the enemy so he would flee. *"Submit yourselves, then, to God. Resist the devil, and he will flee from you."* (James 4:7) *"Resist him, standing firm in the faith, because you know that your brothers throughout the world are undergoing the same kind of sufferings."* (I Peter 5:9)
4. I claimed victory and thanked God for what He had done and was doing in this trial. *"Whoever claims to live in him must walk as Jesus did."* (I John 2:6)

The second day, I was running and talking with God. Again, I asked Him to take my thoughts captive (because, again, my own thoughts were not serving me well.). I also asked God to speak to me.

This time, He said, *"The devil is betting you'll quit."*

I didn't know it at the time, but I made a fatal mistake. I didn't see it until I was talking with another Warrior Mom about it. I thought that I had followed Steps 1-4 above, but I hadn't. I added a provoking element. I actually tapped the devil on the shoulder and said, "Oh, yeah?!" (Remember how I focused on telling you not to say a slanderous word to the enemy? (Jude 1:8) It went something like this:

SKIT
Don't Bet on It!

Me: A woman who is writing this handbook and who realizes that she provoked the enemy
Bren: The friend who informs me that we are not supposed to say a slanderous word to the enemy

[BEGIN SCENE]

Me: "Yeah, Bren, I was really under attack, but I quoted scripture and praised God and really fussed the devil out yesterday! It was great and I won!"

Bren: "Kristina, I'm not sure, but I think I just read somewhere: aren't we not supposed to say slanderous things to the enemy? I think even the archangel, Michael, didn't say bad things to him."

Me: "What? I don't know, but I didn't "really" fuss him out, I just did Steps 1-4."

Bren: "Well, okay. I'm not trying to hurt your feelings or anything. It's just that I think I just read about this very topic somewhere in my Bible."

Me: "No, I'm not offended. Well, maybe I did get a little big-headed. We should probably look into this."

Bren: "I'll try to find where I read that. I just read it."

TWO DAYS LATER

Me: "Bren, I found it! It's in Jude 1:8-10: *In the very same way, these dreamers pollute their own bodies, reject authority and slander celestial beings. But even the archangel Michael, when he was disputing with the devil about the body of Moses did not dare to bring a slanderous accusation against him, but said, "The Lord rebuke you!" Yet these men speak abusively against whatever they do not understand; and what things they do understand by instinct, like unreasoning animals–they are the very things that destroy them.*

Bren: "That's right. I remember reading that. Just the other day, I was drawn to Jude. I don't know why, but I was thinking that I had never read it, and it's such a short book. I wondered what was in it. I remember now."

Me: "That's so interesting. I wonder why the warrior angel, Michael, didn't fuss him out? He's the warrior angel, after all. But I guess, Jesus didn't even say bad things to him. You would think if anyone is going to do it, it would be Jesus."

Bren:	"Yep, Jesus just constantly resisted him. The devil always came around and tempted Jesus, but Jesus didn't go around hunting him down to pick a fight with him. He just went about His Father's business, and then resisted the enemy when he came around to tempt him."
Me:	"Yeah, and interestingly enough, it's just like what we were talking about before, the way that Jesus finally won the war against the enemy was not to fight but to sacrifice His life! Wow! This is really huge."
Bren:	"Yeah, it's awesome isn't it?"
Me:	"You know, Bren, I was big-headed. I actually picked a fight with the enemy! He was giving me little battles, provoking me and wearing me out. But, when God told me that the devil was betting I'd quit, the devil wasn't tempting me or even bothering me at that moment. The devil was betting I'd quit to God, but he wasn't messing with me. I actually went and tapped the devil on the shoulder and said, 'Oh, yeah?!' Gees, I provoked the enemy, and I wasn't even thinking about how the enemy loves to try to prove himself. I brought a nuke upon myself!"
Bren:	"Wow. That's what happened. You were just supposed to resist the enemy and he would have had to flee, but you fell into *The Tennis Match* trap with him and then he put his tennis balls down and nuked you with a basketball!"
Me:	"So, we're supposed to deal with what is allowed to come our way, but we don't go seeking it out! Take gangs, for example. I know they're there and they are probably doing something criminal, but I don't take it upon myself to go down a dark alley and say, 'Hey, gang members, you shouldn't be doing that!' I'd be targeted! And it's not even my job to stop the gang members; that's what the cops are for!"
Bren:	[laugh] "Yep, and really, God is the cop in situations with the enemy. Ultimately it's His war anyway, and He's already won. And as Warrior Moms, we are supposed to be prepared for the battles and wars that are brought to us, but we still have to entrust God with them. I guess we can get big-headed in our warriorness and actually shoot ourselves in the foot! It would be just like the enemy to use our Warrior Mom lessons against us.
	"Wow, it's as if we have to constantly be aware that we can get arrogant at the drop of a hat, and that kind of spiritual ignorance is like kryptonite to us.

Me: So, let's review what we have learned.
1. Warrior Moms must understand the armor of God because we must be protected in battles and wars against us.
2. Warrior Moms must be nourished in the fruit of the Spirit.
3. Battles come, followed by a nuke attack.
4. Sacrifice is the ultimate way to win.
5. We don't seek out battles and wars. We just resist and stand firm in the ones presented to us."

Bren: Yep, and that fifth one is huge!"

Me: "Yeah, it's really huge because I'm writing this study, and I almost didn't know about number five. I would have led a bunch of women into an ambush! If I got them all ready to fight and full of spiritual adrenaline, they would have tapped the enemy on the shoulder like I did! That would have been as smart as seeking out gangs, and they would have gotten massacred in a war that they shouldn't have been in to begin with! Can you imagine the destruction and devastation?! The enemy almost tricked me. Thank God, God revealed that to us. Thank God you said something to me about Jude!"

Bren: "Yeah, and I wasn't trying to hurt your feelings or insult you, but I just felt like there was something to it."

Me: "And you were right! And I'm not offended. Maybe I was a little defensive at first, but I guess I was surprised at what you were saying. Maybe I was taken aback because I was thinking, 'I wasn't being arrogant. I was just doing what I'm supposed to do: Steps 1–4,' but I was actually being big-headed, and I'm so glad you pointed that out. I could have led tons of women into an ambush!"

Bren: "Thank God we know, and to think I thought I was just curiously reading Jude. God was showing me that so I could tell you about it."

Me: "Yeah, we're supposed to be equipped and prepared, but we don't run down a hill like Walter Wallace (Mel Gibson's role) in *Braveheart* and say, 'Bring it on enemy!' We're supposed to stand firm and fight the good fight, but we must never lose sight of the fact that the battle is not ours, but God's" (II Chronicles 20:15).

[END OF SCENE]

Warrior Moms, get this concept in your core. Resist the enemy and he will flee; don't tap him on the shoulder and say slanderous things to him. Remember *The Tennis Match*; it applies to the physical world and the spiritual world.

I would like to address something you're probably wondering about. How do you know which battles are yours and which ones aren't? I have a short and important answer: Pray. More than likely the battles that present themselves on the front lawn or in the living room of your life (figuratively and literally speaking) are yours. There may be battles that aren't so obvious that God wants you to join in as well. Spend time in His Word and with Him, and God will reveal those to you. Don't be a busy body and think it's up to little 'ol you to save the world and get involved in everyone's business. These types of women are difficult to be around. Personally, I haven't been compelled to contribute positively to the kingdom of God when I'm around them. Although, I must admit, my patience-muscle gets a good workout. Thessalonians 4:11 reads, *"Make it your business to lead a quiet life, to mind your own business and to work with your hands, just as we told you so that your daily life may win the respect of outsiders . . ."*

Finally, always remember: regarding the battles that God is asking you to join, it's not up to you to win them. It's up to you to trust God with them and through them. Also, don't let all this knowledge about spiritual warfare freak you out. Remember the Faith Slap versus Freak Out lesson. And just so you know, this stuff has been going on for a long time (Revelation 12). Now that you know about it, you can be prepared for it instead of walking around aimlessly without your armor and without the nourishment of the fruit of the Spirit. Don't be full of fear simply because you know about it now; be the Warrior Mom you have been trained to be! Remember you make a choice as to whether you will live by fear or live by faith.

DONT CONFUSE ALL BATTLES AND WARS AS YOURS

FIELD EXERCISES

1. Taking all you've learned into account, what has been the most valuable lesson?
   _____
   _____
   _____
   _____

2. In what ways have you changed since day one of the study? Email your Warrior Mom Leader to let her know how you have been transformed by the study. Feel free to share your comments or questions with me by emailing me at Kristina@WarriorMoms.net. Let me know if it's OK to use your comments in a future book.
   _____
   _____
   _____
   _____

3. What part of the armor is your favorite? Do you even have a favorite? If not, what do you like best about wearing the armor?
   _____
   _____
   _____

4. What is your favorite fruit? _____

5. Explain how you see the armor and the fruit working together for the Warrior Mom's benefit?
   _____
   _____
   _____

6. What do you do now that you never did before you began the study?
   _____
   _____
   _____

7. List your most recent victory. Explain how it came to pass.

   _____
   _____
   _____

8. Now that you are transformed, how will you share this good news with another woman that you know?

   _____
   _____
   _____

9. Make sure you keep in touch with your fellow Warrior Moms. If you haven't already created a contact list, do so now.

   _____
   _____
   _____

Warrior Moms Unite! ™

www.WarriorMoms.net

THE WARRIOR MOM HANDBOOK

CHAPTER 15

Now that you have reached the end of the handbook, you are fully aware and equipped for battles and wars. You are alert. You are aware of the war that has been waged on women and their offspring (Revelation 12). You understand things on a higher level, and your eyes have been opened to see above the pesky matters of this age. Yes, it will be difficult. Knowing these things doesn't make it easier, but it helps prepare you so that you can endure and be victorious. So many of us think that at a certain point, things will be better, easier, calmer, and/or happier. So many of us have learned to live for a goal only to realize that when we accomplish that goal, we still aren't happy. We discussed the difference between happiness and joy earlier. Don't forget the difference.

With regard to becoming a Warrior Mom, it doesn't mean that things will be easier, better, or fixed. Nope, it simply means that you are equipped. You can defeat the enemy because you understand his tactics against you. You have eyes of faith now. You get it. Don't expect to get to a point of perfection with all of this. Simply expect to persevere through the trials. You are no longer an ignorant turtle without a shell, without armor, and without fruit. You are no longer isolated and defeated. You have met other women who have gone through and are going through the same types of trials. You understand that as soon as you are isolated and alone, you are more susceptible to being defeated. You know that you must stay strong and united with other Warrior Moms.

Ecclesiastes 4:9-12 *Two are better than one, because they have a good return for their work: If one falls down, his friend can help him up. But pity a man who falls and has no one to help him up! Also, if two lie down together, they will keep warm. But how can one keep warm alone! Though one may be overpowered, two can defend themselves. A cord of three strands is not quickly broken.*

I hope that this study is just the beginning of a new way of life for you. May you go forward and teach others what you have learned. Will you lead the next small group of Warrior Moms? There are women all across the world, isolated and defeated within their hearts and homes. May you be the one who knocks on their door and says, "Let me see that disc that you've been playing." And finally, to the women of this study who have sought God and who dared to become Warriors, you can assuredly say: GAME OVER!

Please sign your name on the line below:

_____

Warrior Mom

WELCOME, WARRIOR MOM!

Finally, be strong in the Lord and in his mighty power. Put on the full armor of God so that you can take your stand against the devil's schemes. For our struggle is not against flesh and blood, but against the rulers, against the authorities, against the powers of this dark world and against the spiritual forces of evil in the heavenly realms. Therefore put on the full armor of God, so that when the day of evil comes, you may be able to stand your ground, and after you have done everything, to stand. Stand firm then, with the belt of truth buckled around your waist, with the breastplate of righteousness in place, and with your feet fitted with the readiness that comes from the gospel of peace. In addition to all this, take up the shield of faith, with which you can extinguish all the flaming arrows of the evil one. Take the helmet of salvation and the sword of the Spirit, which is the word of God. And pray in the Spirit on all occasions with all kinds of prayers and requests. With this in mind, be alert and always keep on praying for the saints.
(Ephesians 6:10-18).

But the fruit of the Spirit is love, joy, peace, patience, kindness, goodness, faithfulness, gentleness and self-control.
Against these things there is no law.
Those who belong to Christ have crucified
the sinful nature with its passions and desires.
Since we live by the Spirit,
let us keep in step with the Spirit.
(Galatians 5:22-25)

ABOUT THE AUTHOR

Kristina Seymour lives in Lawrenceville, Georgia, with her husband, Brian, and their two children. She grew up in a small town in the Pacific Northwest and served four years in the United States Air Force. Having earned a Masters degree in Professional Counseling, Kristina is currently working on her Doctorate in Clinical Psychology. A small group leader at her church, she is passionate about equipping women through the Word. Kristina is also an inspirational speaker. It is her heart's desire to inspire all women to be Warriors!

References

NIV Archaeological Study Bible, 2005, Zondervan, Grand Rapids, Michigan, USA.
Managing your Emotions, Meyer, Joyce, 1997, Warner Books Edition, Fenton, Missouri, USA.
The Five Love Languages, Chapman, Gary, 1995, Northfield Publishing, Chicago, Illinois, USA.
The Prayer of Jabez, Wilkinson, Bruce, 2000, Multnomah Publishers Inc., Sisters, Oregon, USA.
Webster Comprehensive Dictionary, Encyclopedia Edition, Volume II, Marckwardt, Cassidy,
    McMillan, 1992, J.G. Ferguson Publishing Company, Chicago, Illinois, USA.

COMING SOON BY KRISTINA SEYMOUR

Through *The Warrior Mom Handbook*, I know you have experienced the transforming power of God's Word in your life as a mom. Now, *The Warrior Wife Handbook* will take you to a new place of intimacy with God. In turn, you will reach a new level of intimacy with your husband.

Intimacy in marriage requires more than a quick conversation over a cup of coffee; it requires Christ at the center of two servant-minded hearts. If you are thinking, "Well, this will never work because I'm the only one who will be reading this book, and if it requires two servant-like hearts, I may as well watch TV too," I read your mind. My response to your thoughts is this: God told **me** to make my husband a sandwich 13 years ago and it revolutionized **our** marriage! In fact, if I had to summarize *The Warrior Wife Handbook* into one profound piece of marriage advice I would tell you four words that God told me, "*Make him a sandwich.*" But, I love to talk more than four words worth; the result is *The Warrior Wife Handbook*.

Throughout the book, I am going to relate each armor and fruit concept to being a wife as unto the Lord. I will speak to you - woman to woman and wife to wife. I will incorporate mistakes I've made, things I've learned, how God has changed me over the last 19 years of marriage, and how I pray for Him to continually grow me up in love. My good friend, Dawn Allen, Ph.D. will be joining us, providing God inspired lessons applicable for any stage of your life and marriage. We will also incorporate insights and lessons from other Warrior Wives.

The Warrior Wife Handbook aims to minister to, equip, and encourage you in your marriage. Through studying His Word, God has created a tenderness in my heart that has caught me slightly off guard and rendered me a new student to the beautiful task of service, love, and rekindled passion for God and His will in my marriage.

As you read, you will recognize two key principles: One - we find our strength from the Word, which is God (John 1:1), and two - being united with other believers (especially other wives in the Word) ensures there will be someone to help us up when we stumble (Ecclesiastes 4:10). As you turn your focus toward God and reflect on lessons learned, I guarantee something will begin to happen in you: You will be prepared to receive all God has for you as you boldly love, and begin to serve with a new found passion.

Remember, Jesus came to serve, and He did it with unfettered dedication and heart-felt concern for all whom He laid His eyes upon. My prayer is that as you lay your eyes upon your husband, while he sleeps, when he rises, when he returns from his day, and all the moments in between that he would sense the Christ-like compassion and passion from you that would rekindle the spark between you seven times seven!

As you delve into *The Warrior Wife Handbook*, you will realize that you are no longer fighting merely with your husband in front of you or with the woman in the mirror. We do not fight with flesh and blood, but with the spiritual forces of evil in the heavenly realms (Ephesians 6:10-18). Just as He did for me, God will step in and you will hear Him say, "*Are you ready to love and be loved as you never have before?*"

The *Warrior Wife Handbook* is for wives who seek God and who dare to become Warrior Wives. The battle is on and to the enemy's plot against your marriage, God says: GAME OVER!

Visit www.WarriorMoms.net to learn more.

*As a Warrior Mom, I have learned that obedience is
not about how I feel; rather, it is about my faith in Him.
I now know that I am a vehicle through which He works.
My job is to simply show up and let Him work. When I do that,
an amazing thing happens: the pressure is off of me and
my attention is diverted from my weakness or inability.
Then, look out! Once I turn my focus on Him and
His power, the sky is the limit and victory is imminent!
There's Strong. Then There's God-Strong!*

*God put a great Warrior Mom team together to bring you
the best possible handbook we could muster. Kristina
and I watched with awe as God worked. We pray you'll be
richly blessed by this study. To God be the glory!*

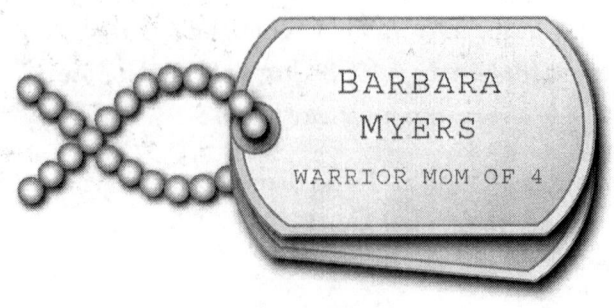

EPHESIANS 6:10-18 & GALATIANS 5:22-23

CERTIFICATE OF COMPLETION

WARRIOR MOM® TRAINING

This certificate is awarded to

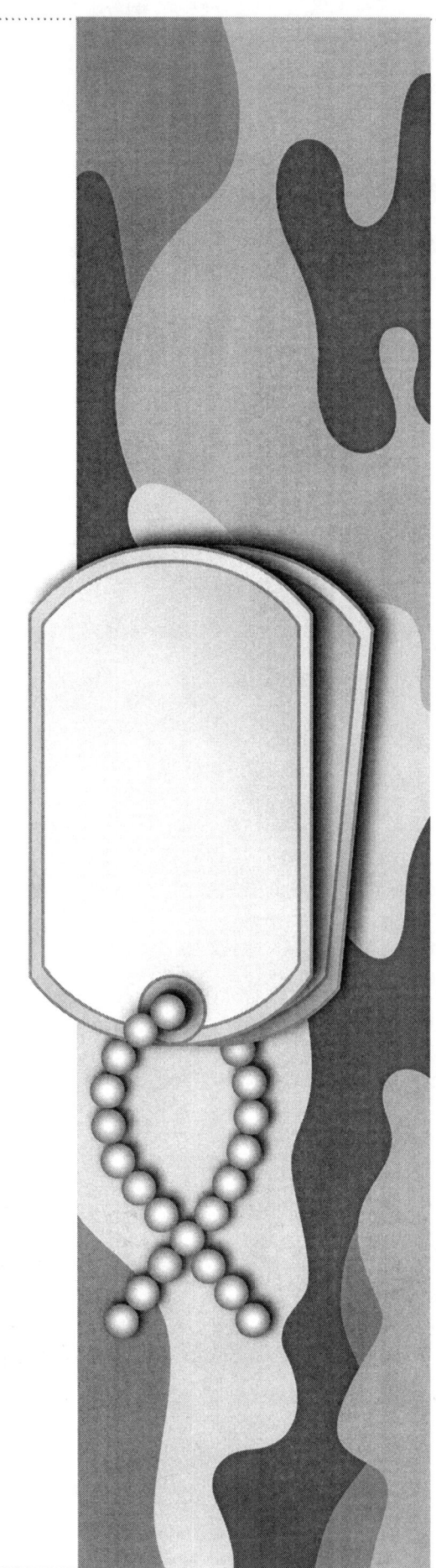

In recognition of being equipped in the Word and relying on God's strength to win everyday battles.

Kristina Seymour

Warrior Mom Founder   Date

_____
Warrior Mom Signature   Date

WARRIOR MOMS UNITE!™

CPSIA information can be obtained at www.ICGtesting.com
Printed in the USA
BVOW06s1746010415

394269BV00002B/25/P